Design Style

Published by Duck Farm Press
PO Box 3073
Robertson NSW
Australia 2577

ISBN: 978-0-6456524-9-9

*I*ntroduction to Design Style

I have a Pinterest page called 'Design Style- Examples of great design everywhere'. It is very eclectic: stones, jewellery, knitwear, old tools, pottery, nature, snakes, poultry, birds, gardens, embroidery, fabrics, wallpaper and houses. You can see from this page that I like colour: bright, contrasting colours. But I also love the drama of black on white.

My drawings vacillate from black on white to colour, but the colour is always bright. Well nearly always. There are a few drawings in this book which show the subtleties of background texture made with common biros.

I often draw without any premonition of what I will draw. I let the shapes dictate how they will sit with each other. Some of the drawings are otherworldly, strange creatures can inhabit this universe. I get inspiration from Nature and from something as utilitarian as the shapes left from a child's wooden toy, the ones that come in flat rectangles and have to be pressed out. These shapes can leave the most interesting negatives behind looking like strange, little caterpillars.

However, I will let the artworks speak their own language to you. For who am I to really interpret them for you? Art is, after all, a connection between the page and the viewer. For then the artist becomes superfluous and the viewer themselves make the art and forge their own reactions to it.
Patricia Lee, April 2023

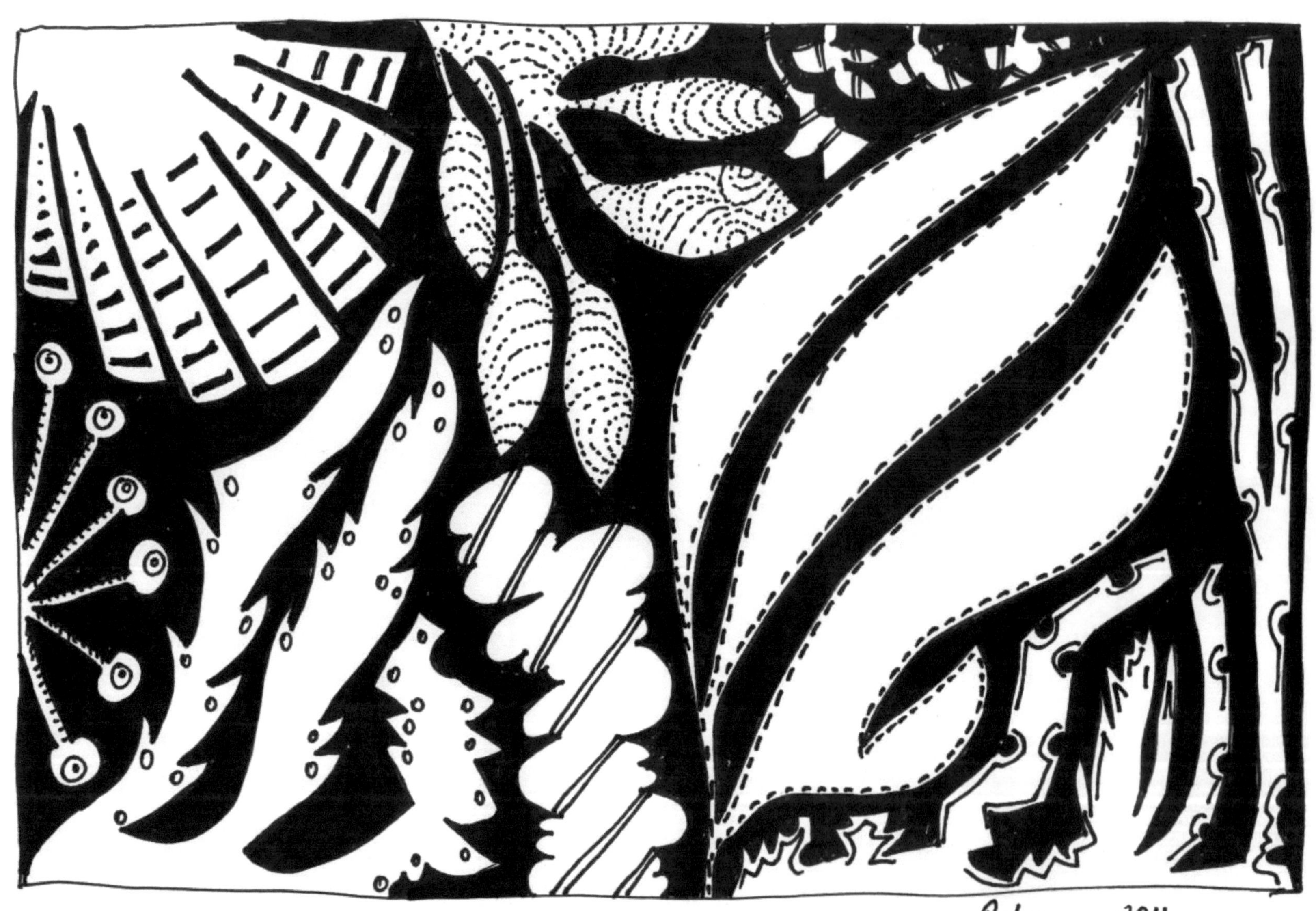
P. Lee   2011

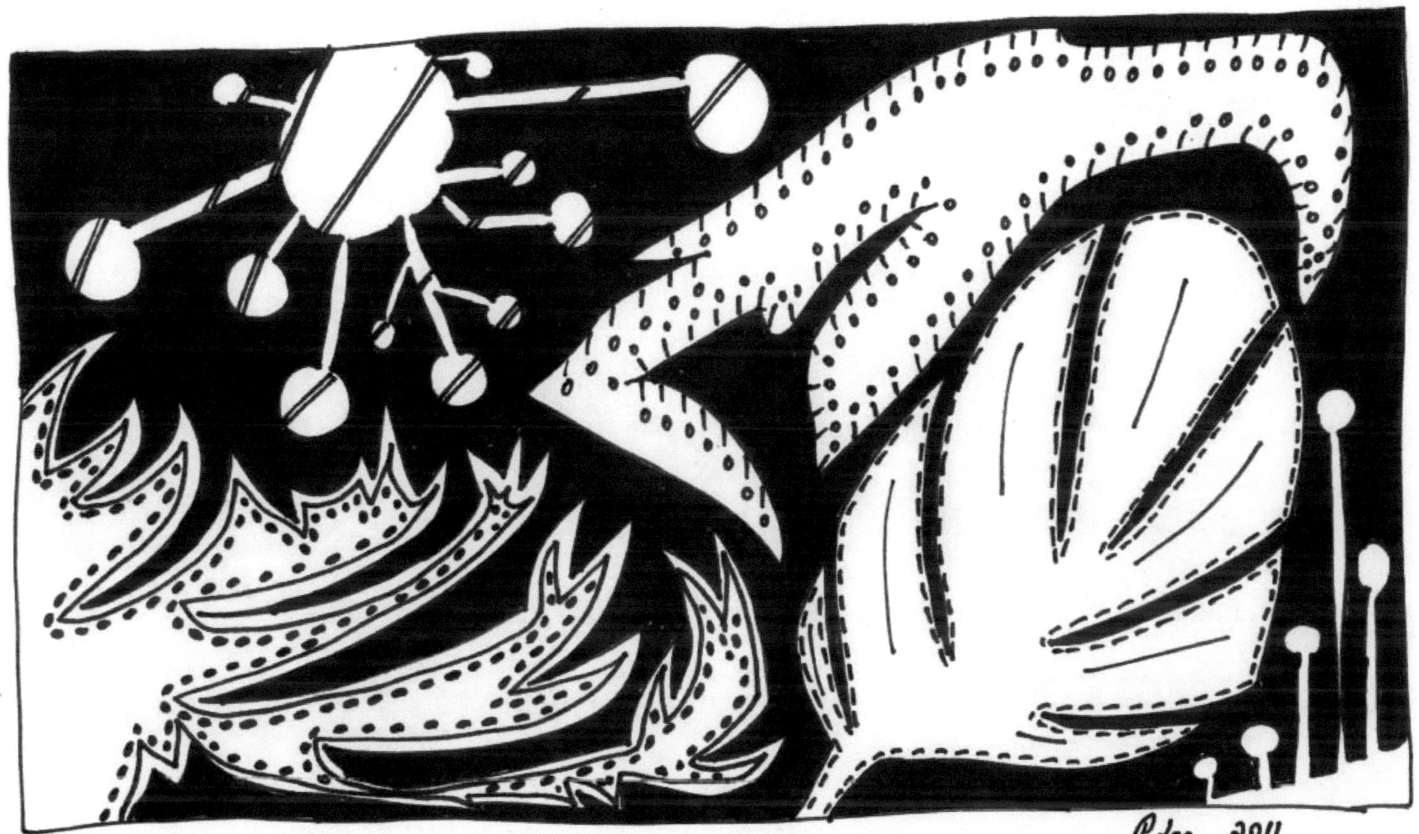
P.Lee 2011

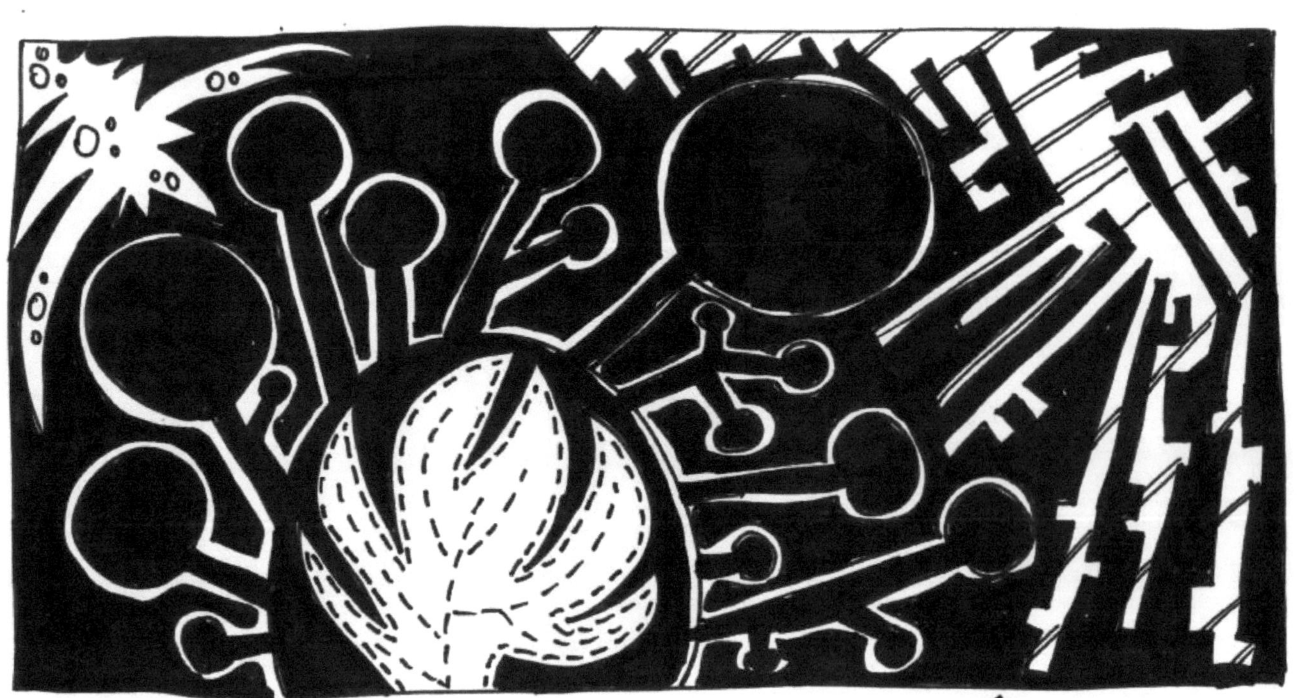

P.Lee 2011

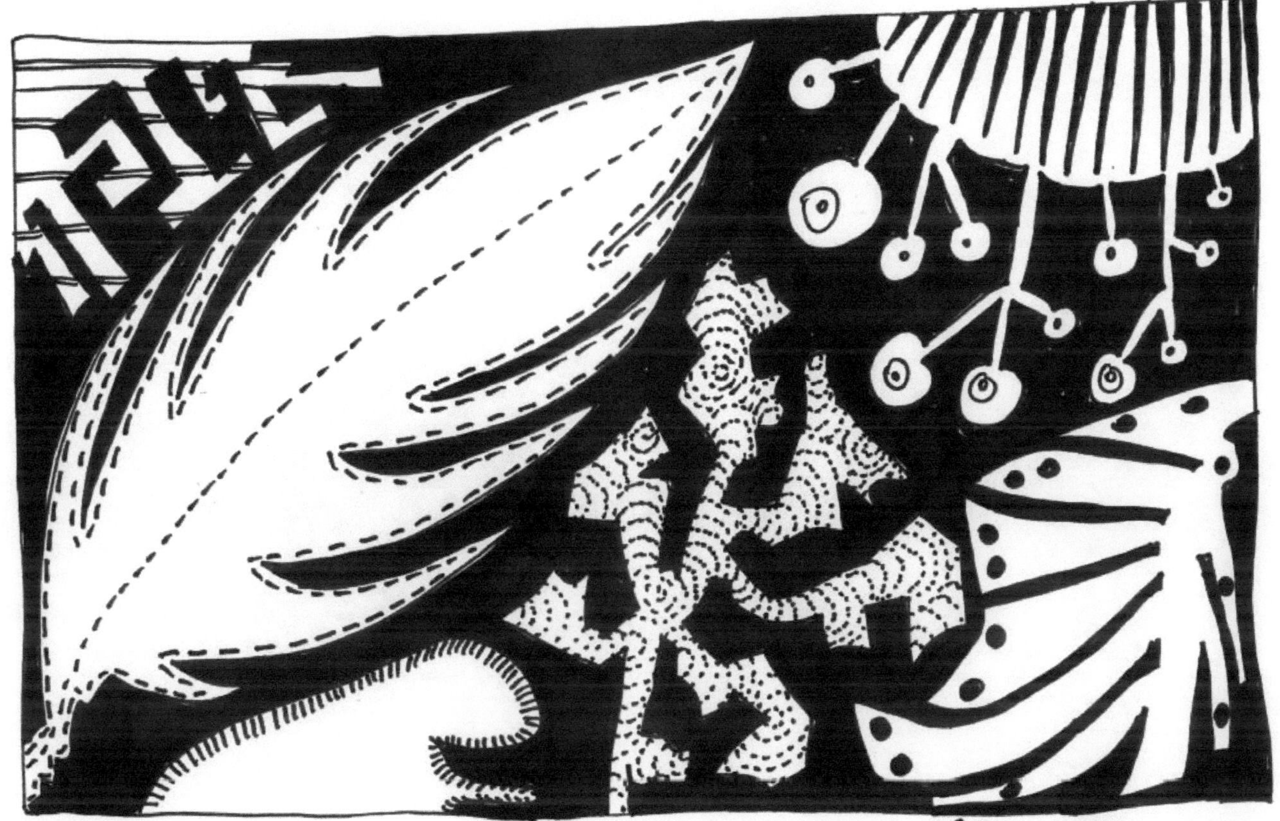

P.Lee. 2011

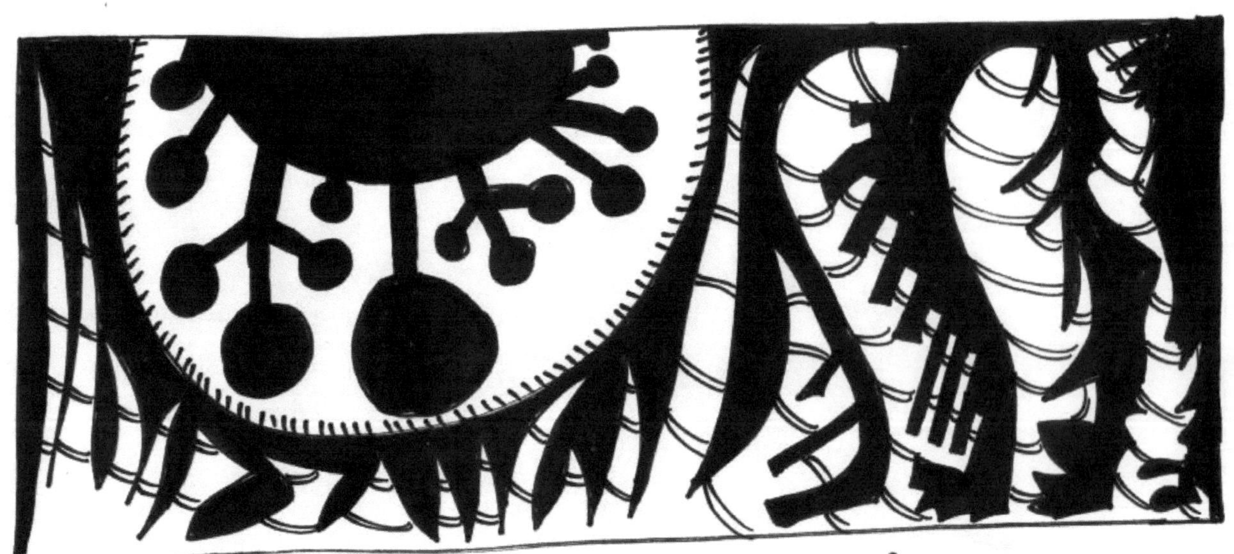

P.Lee 2011

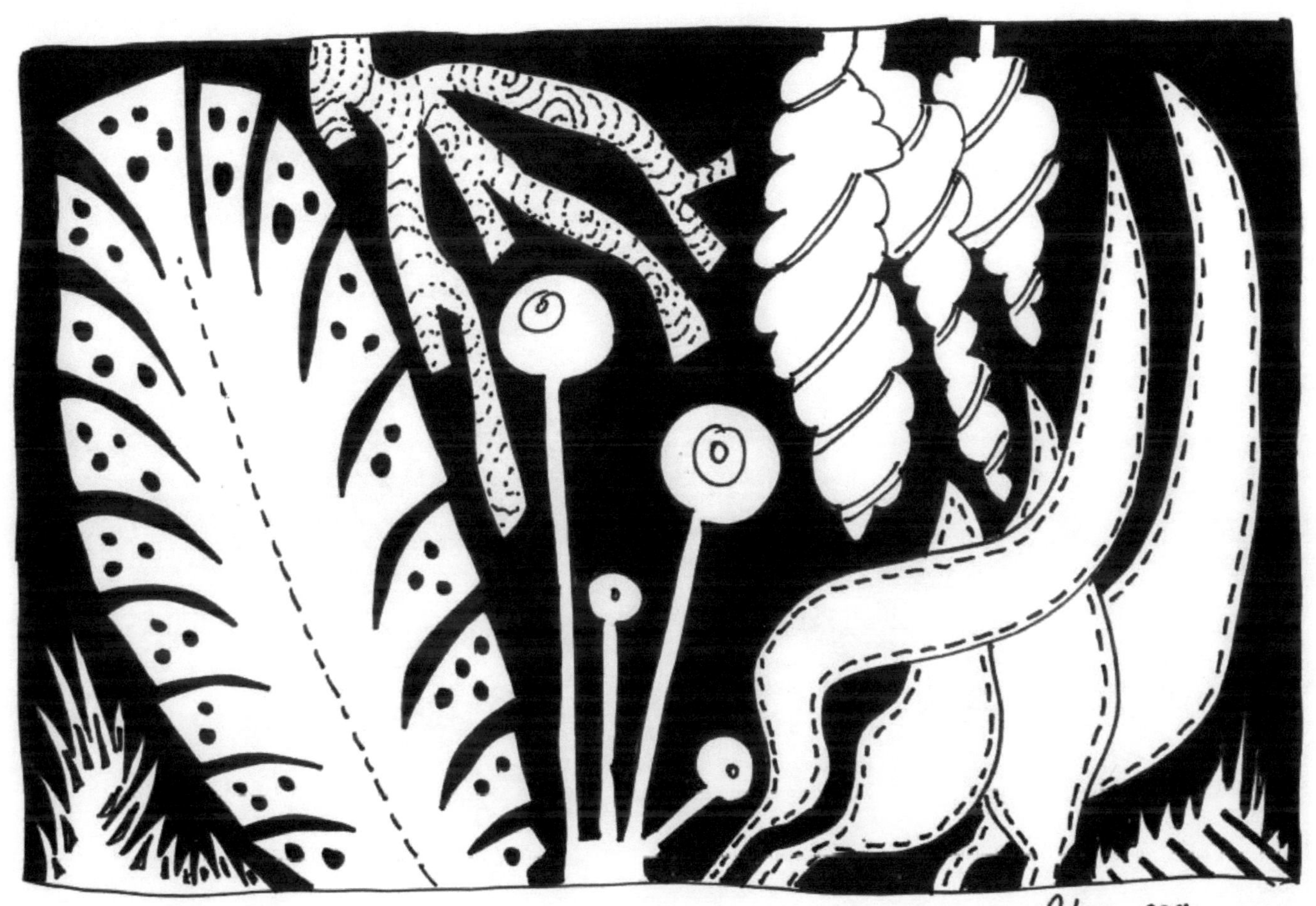
P. Lee 2011

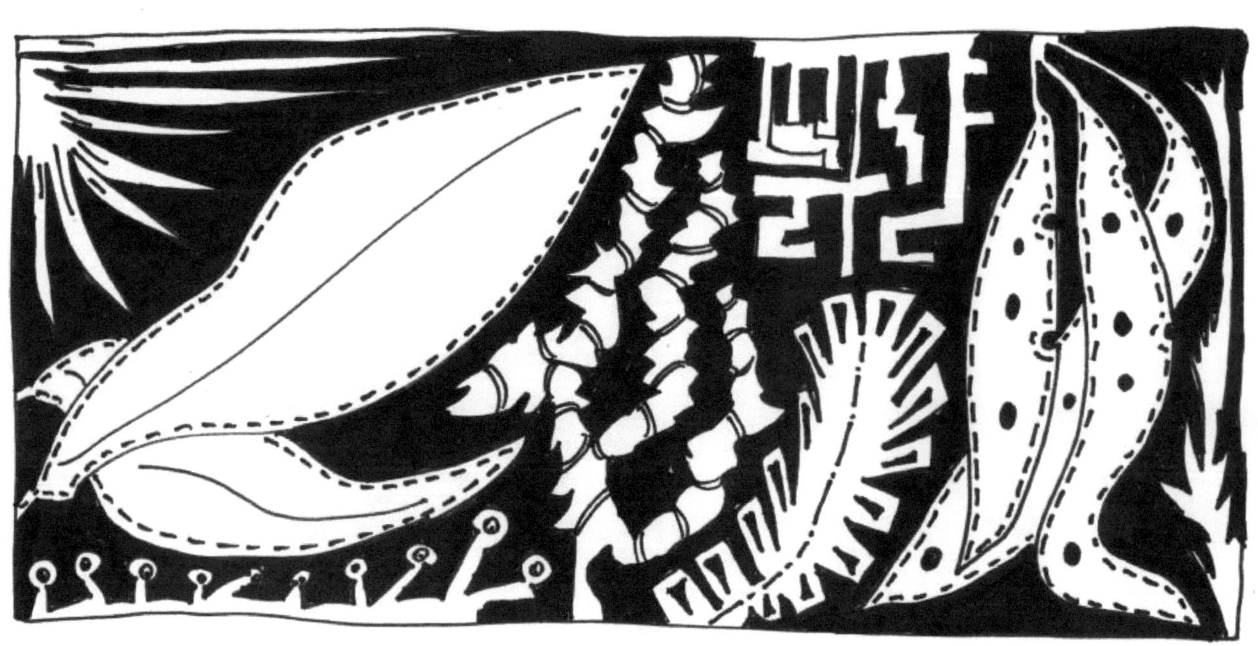

P.Lee 2011

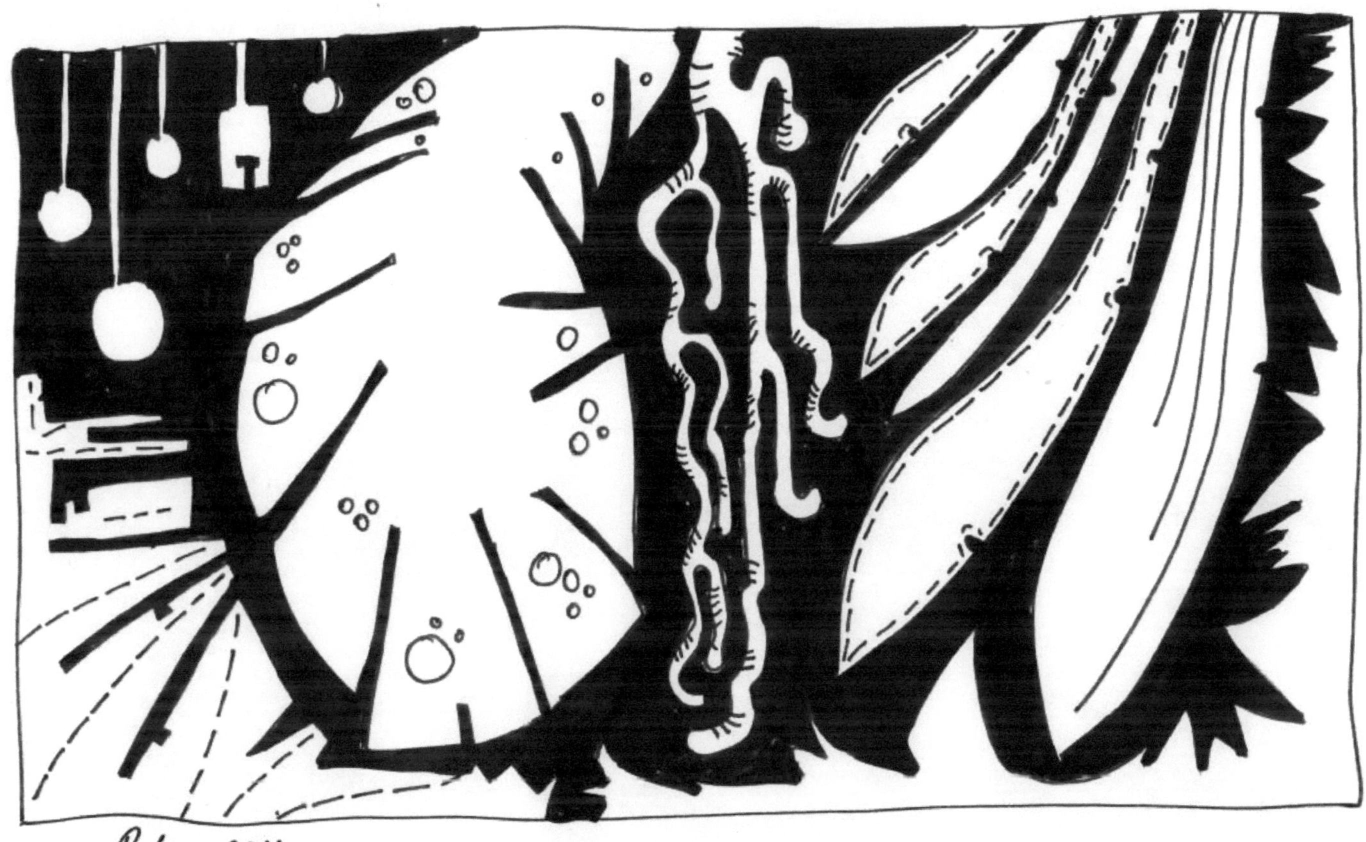

P. Lee 2011

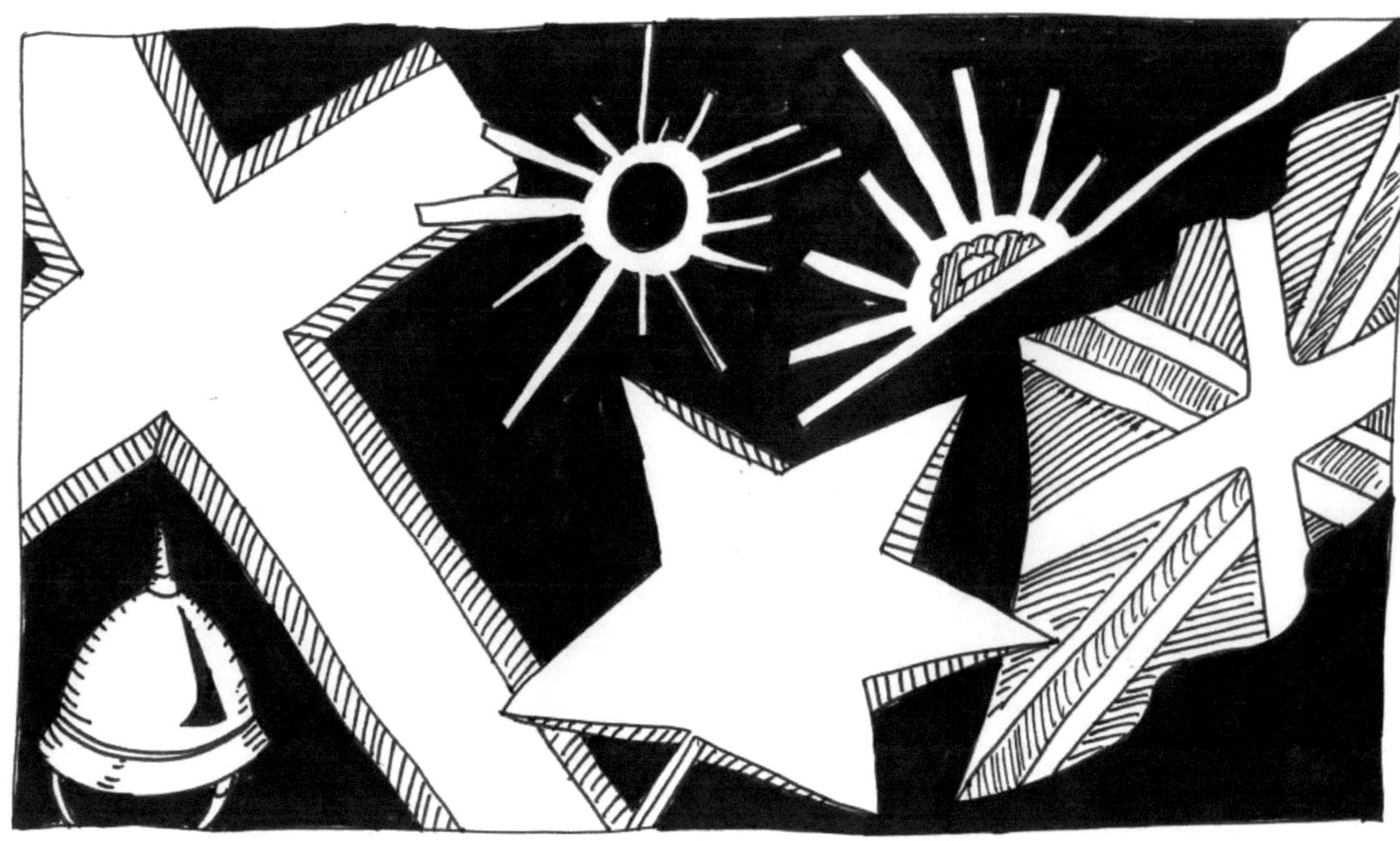

P.lee 2011

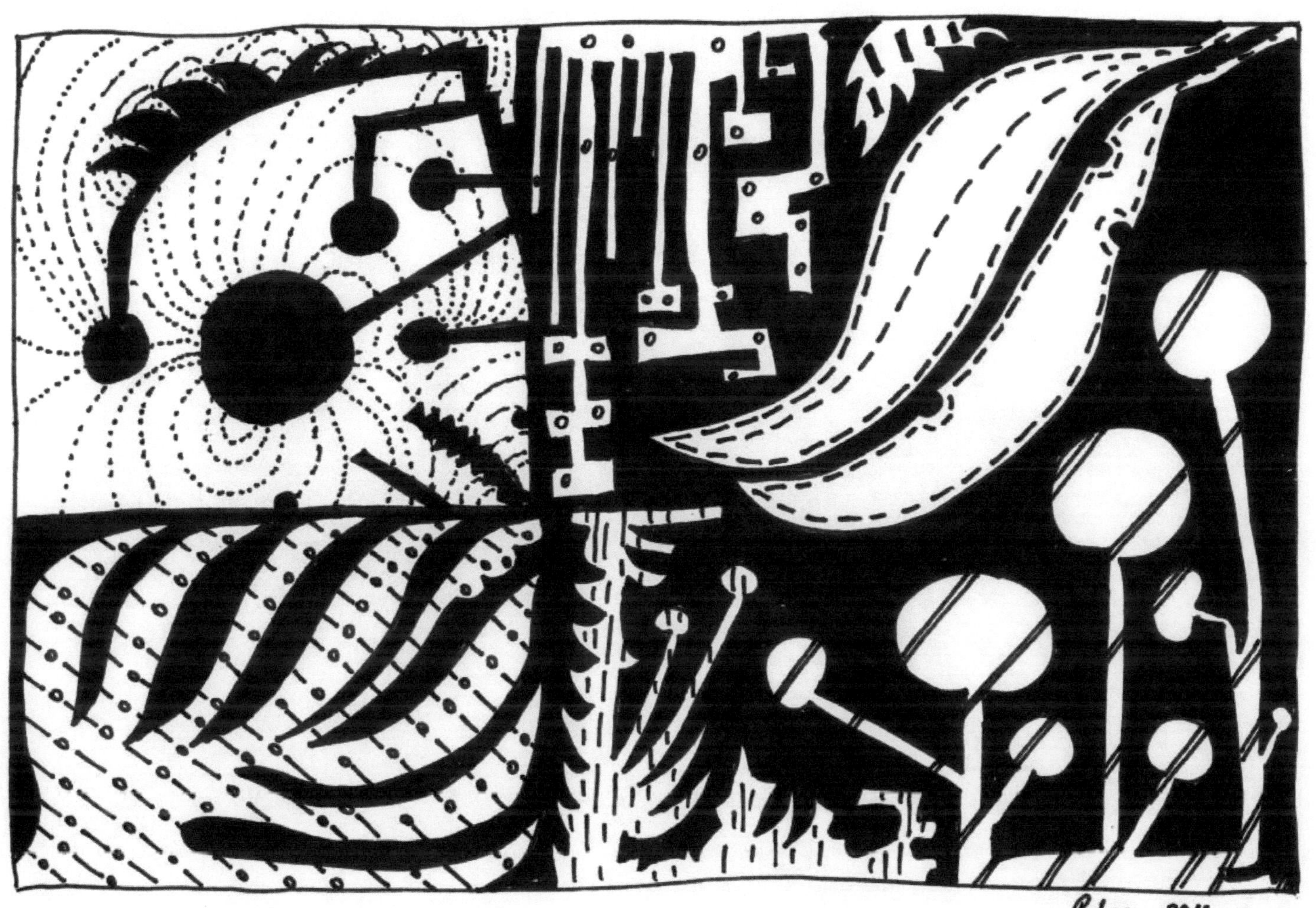

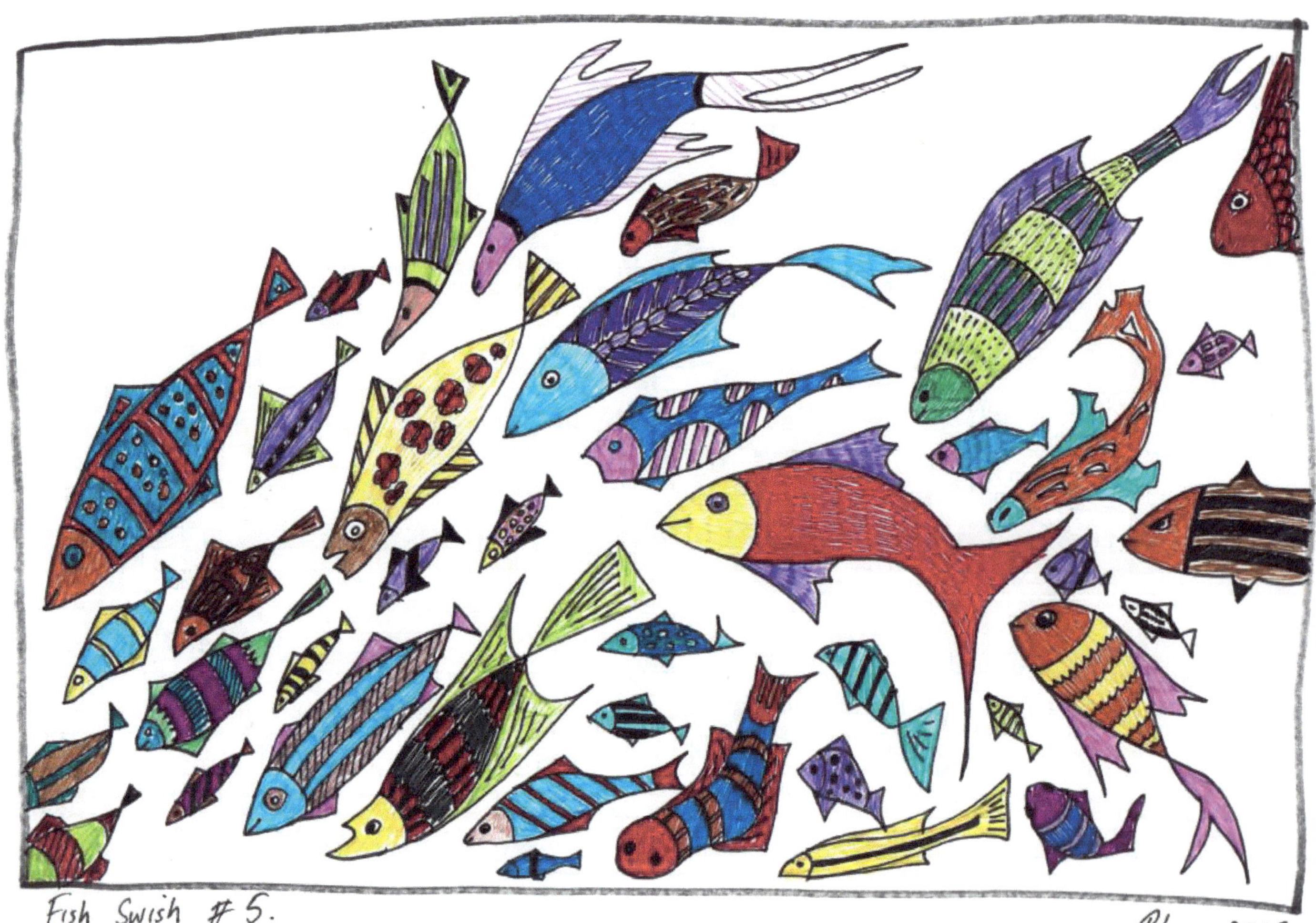

Fish Swish # 5.

PLee 2012.

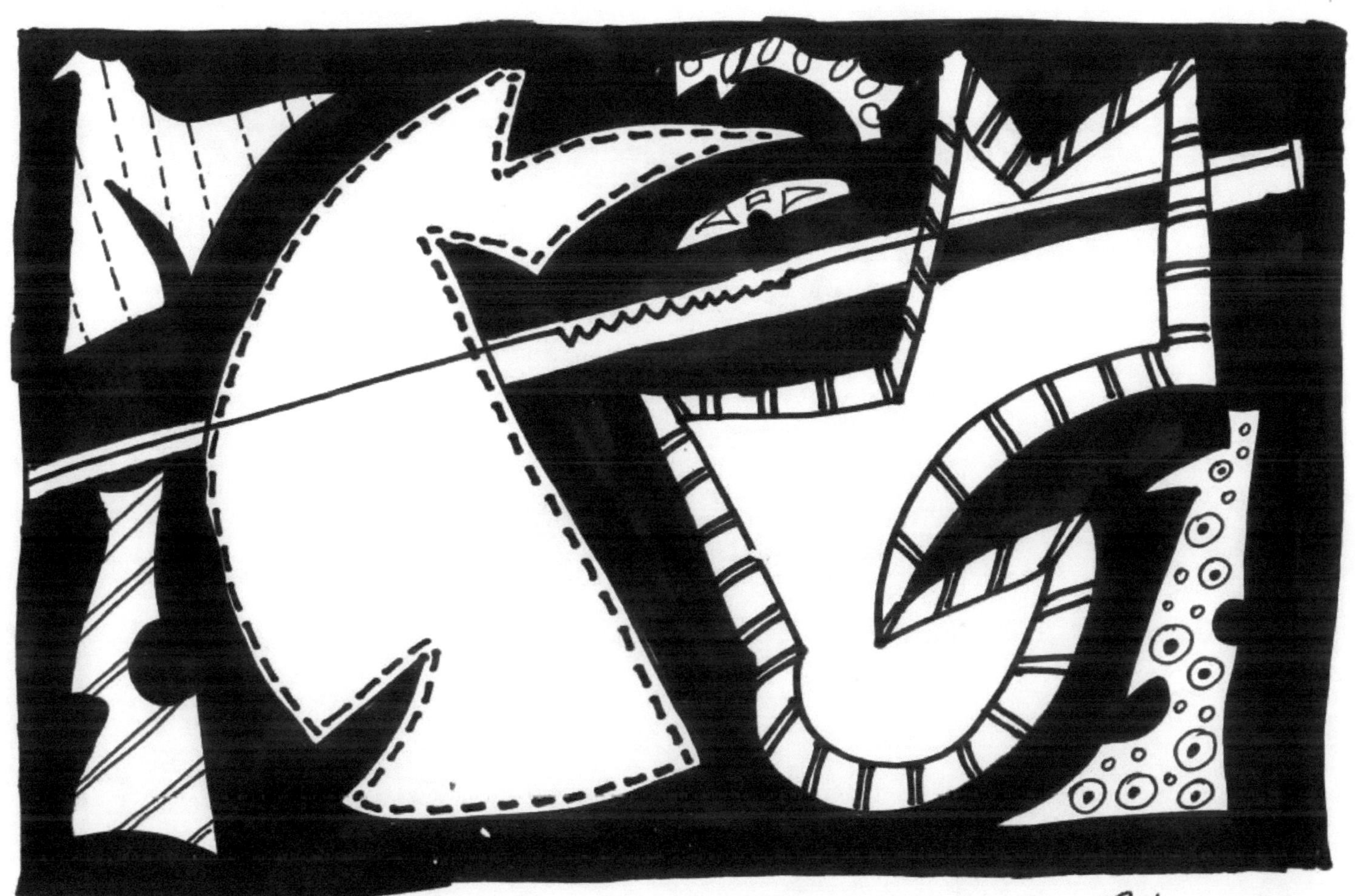

Getting into the rhythm

P. Lee 2013

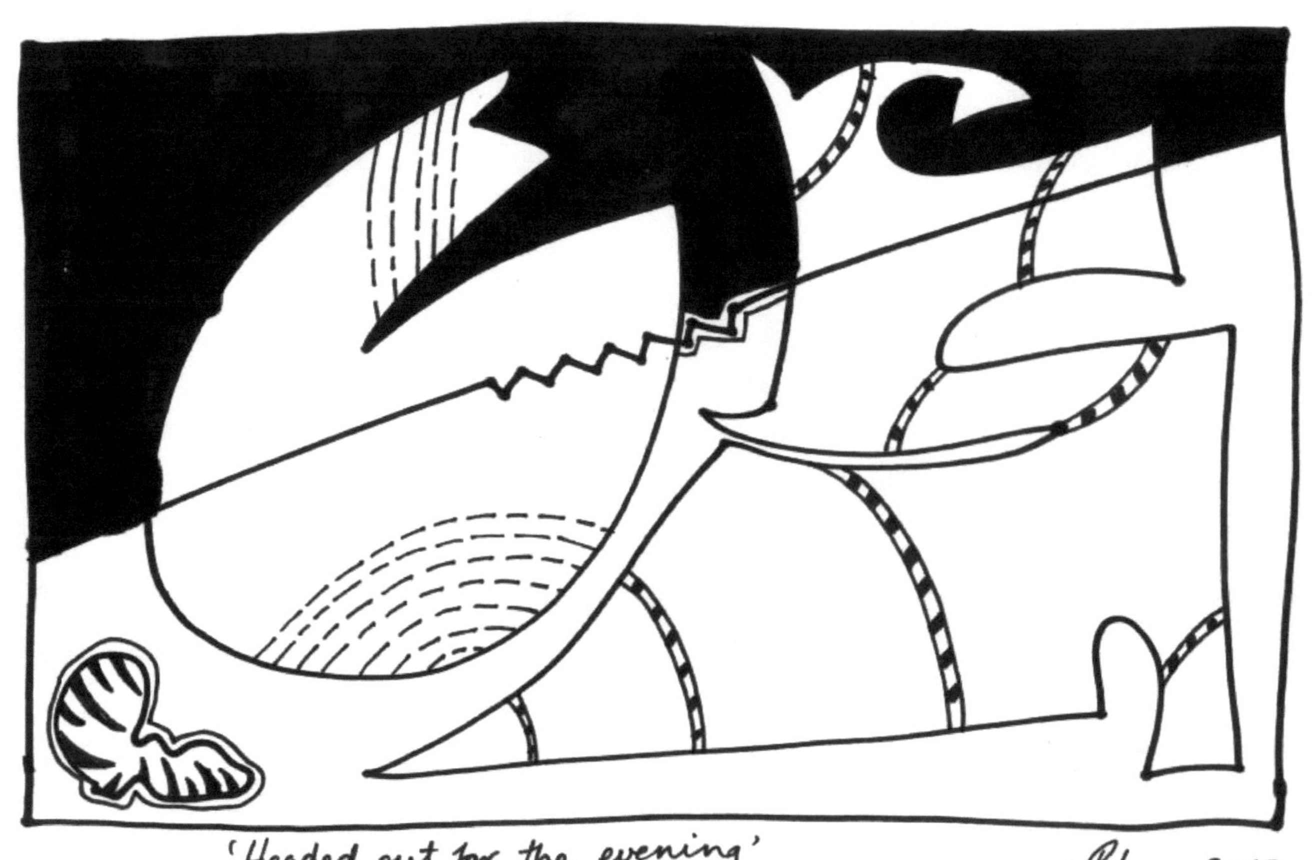

'Headed out for the evening'

P. Lee 2013

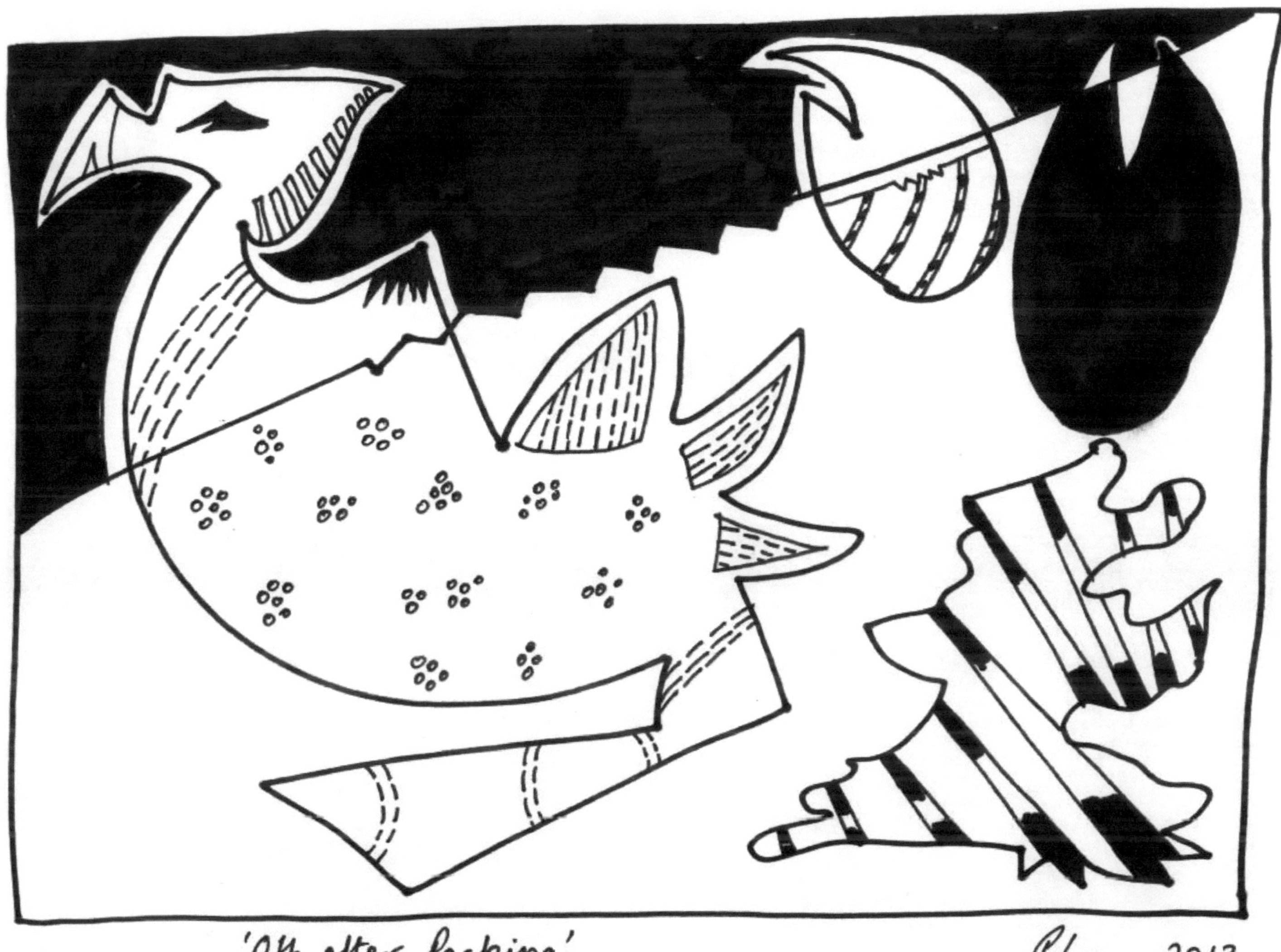

'Off after Packing'.

PdLee 2013

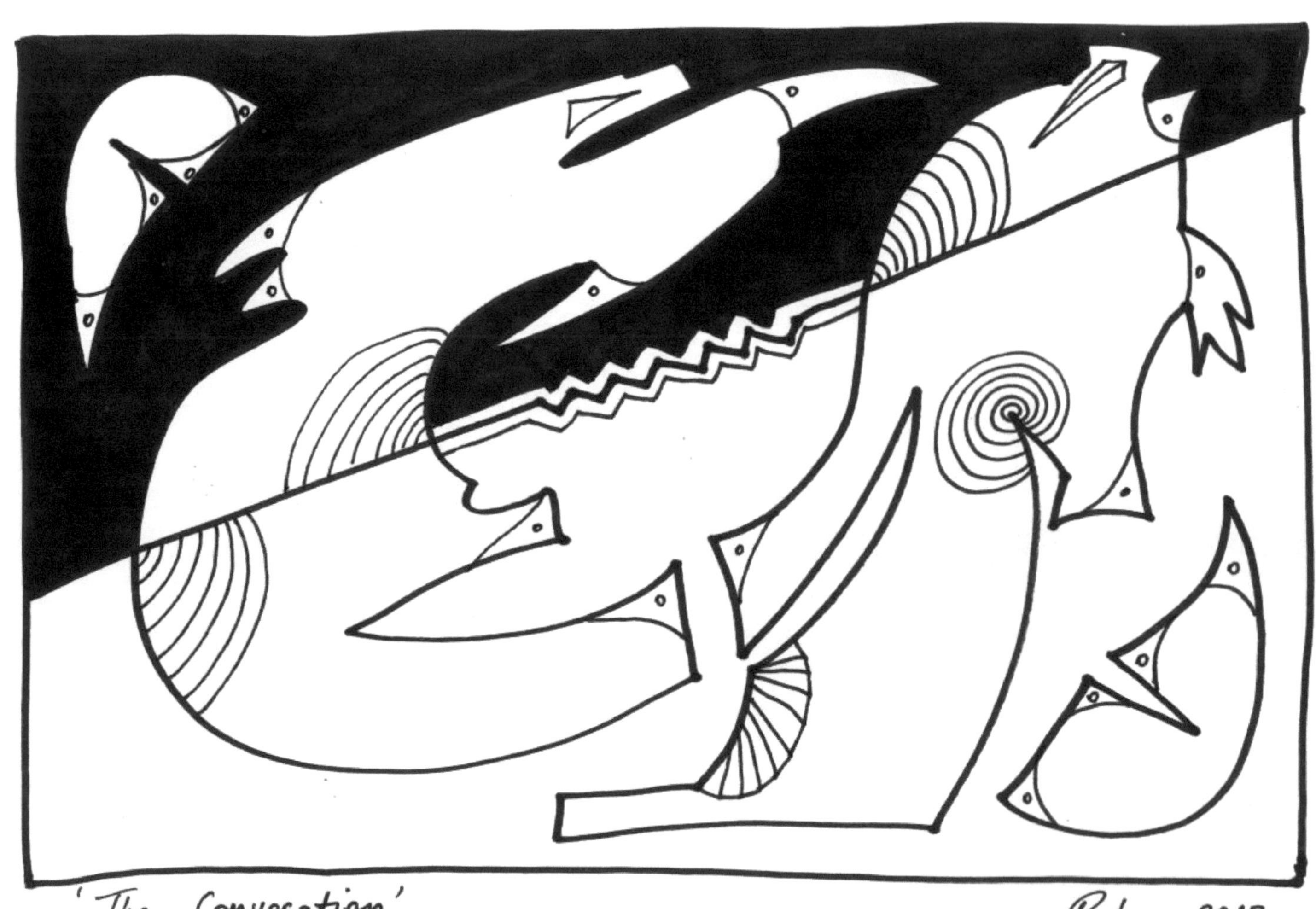

'The Convocation'

P. Lee 2013

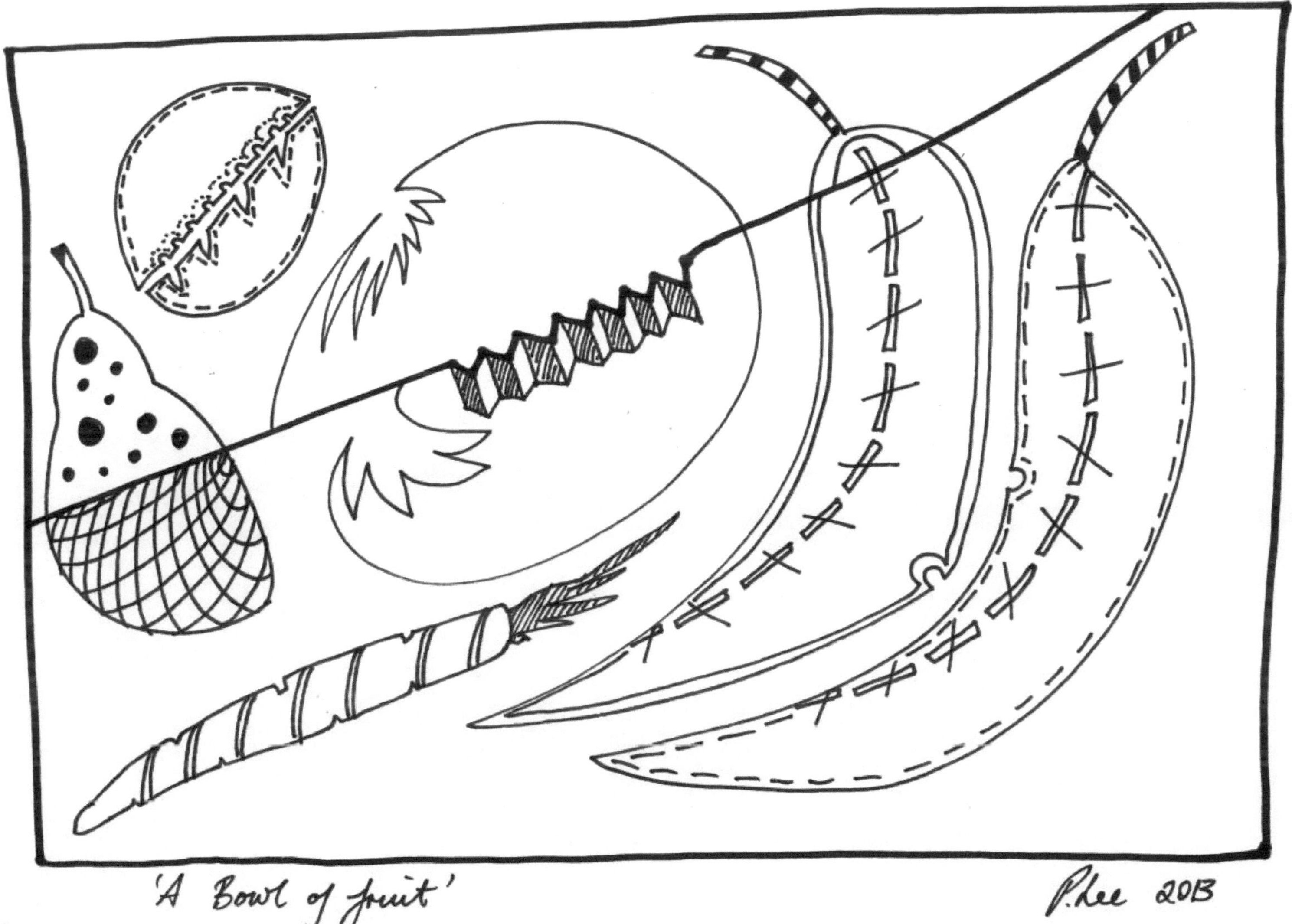

'A Bowl of Fruit'

P. Lee 2013

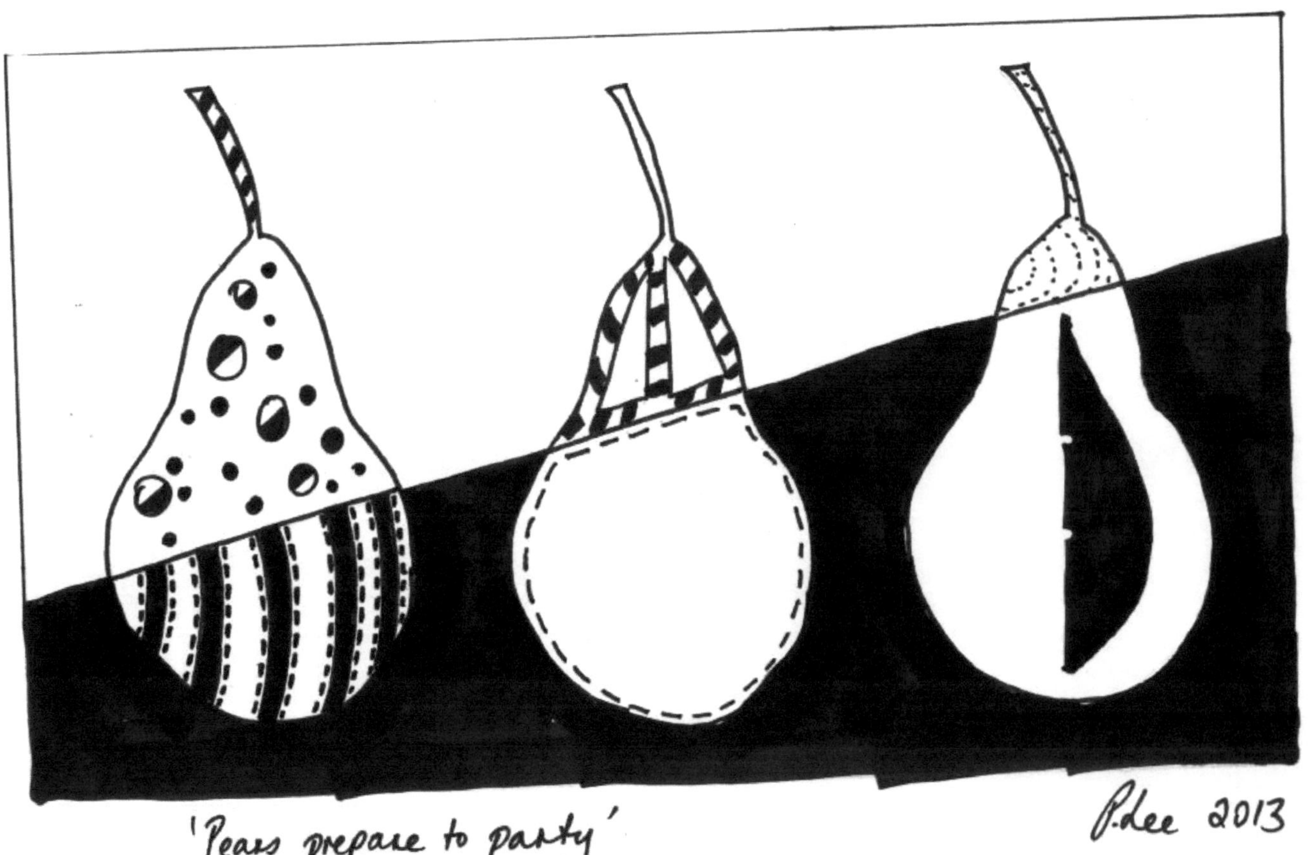

'Pears prepare to party'

P.Lee 2013

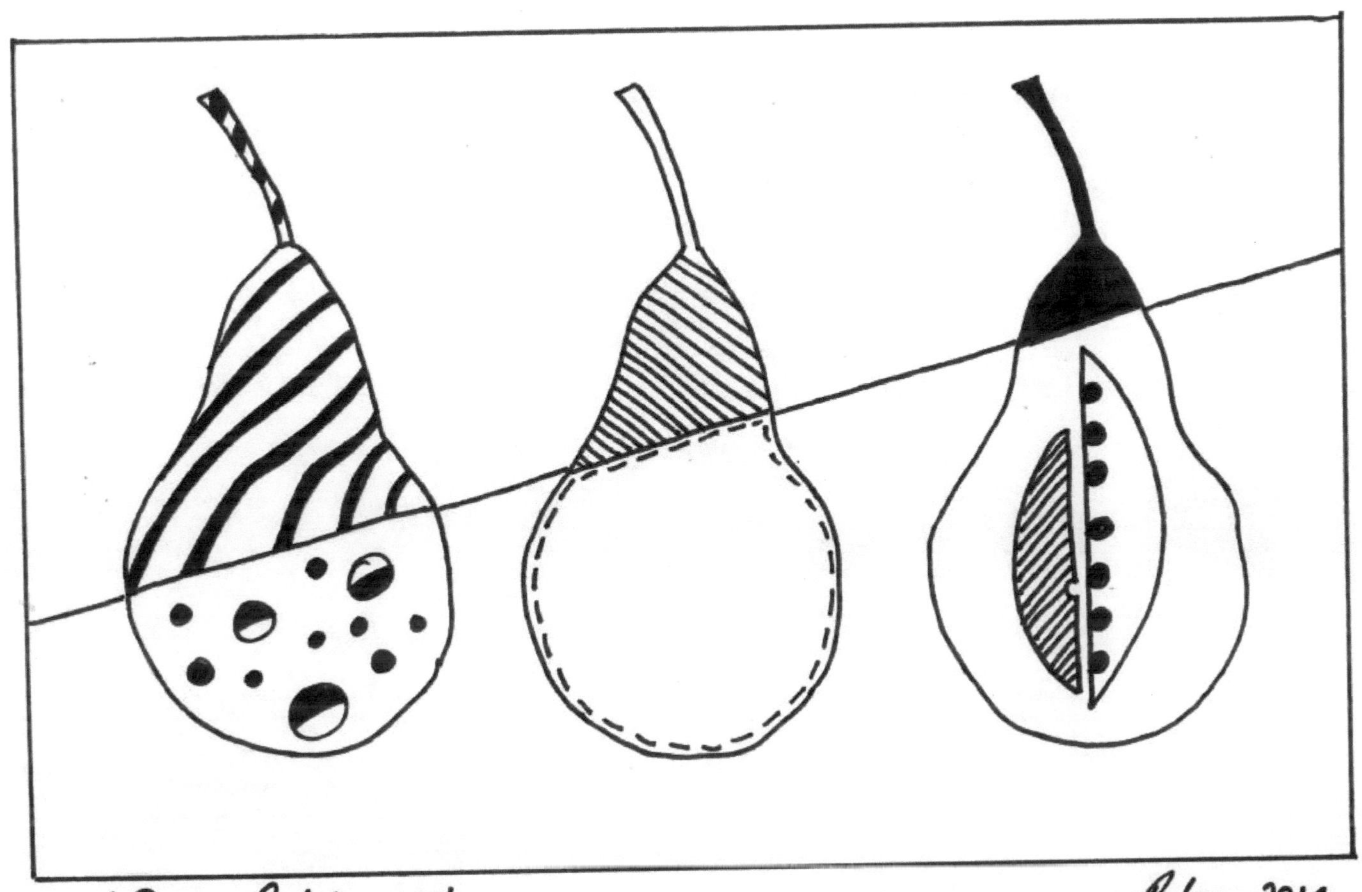

'Pears Patch up'

P.Lee 2014

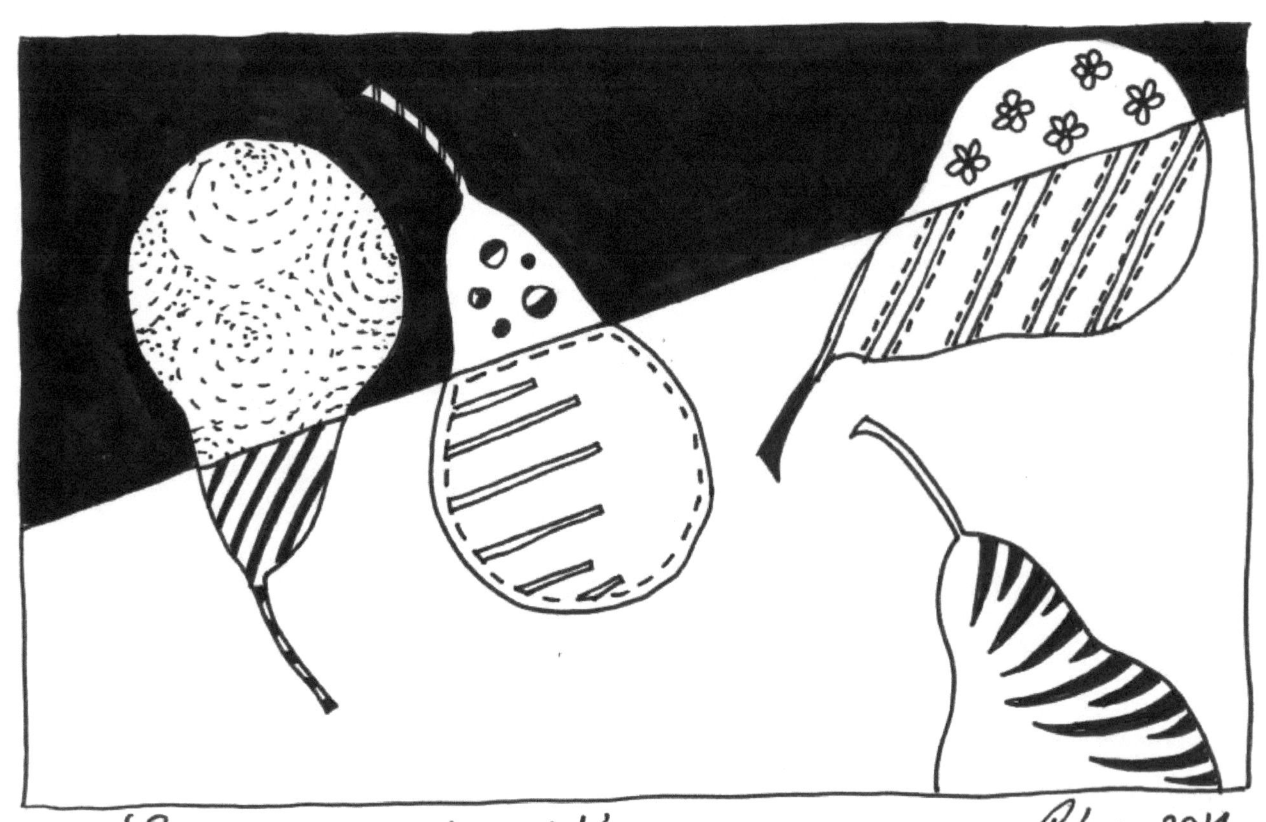

'Pears pause for thought'

P. Lee 2014

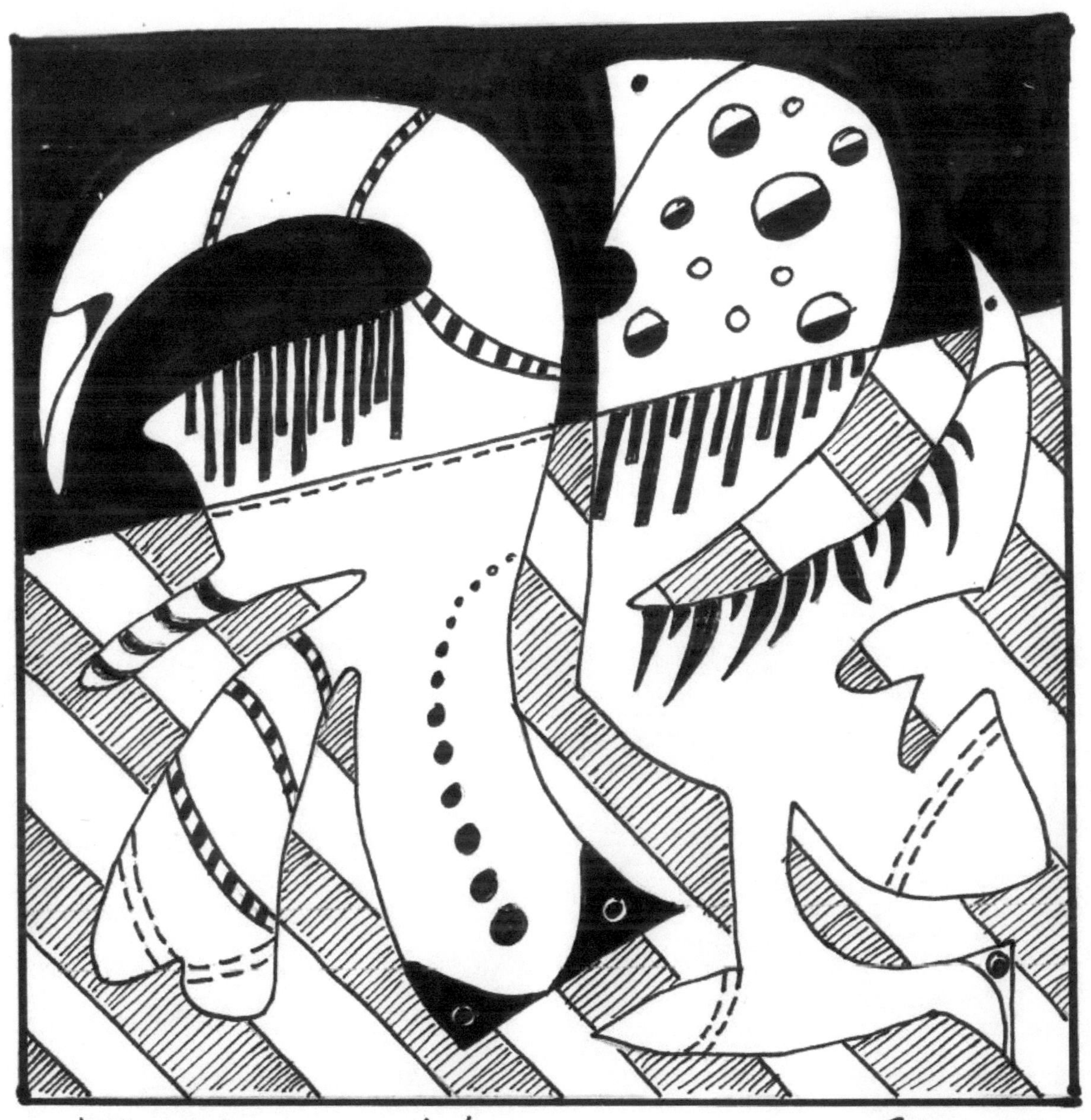

'I told you so!'

P. Lee 2014

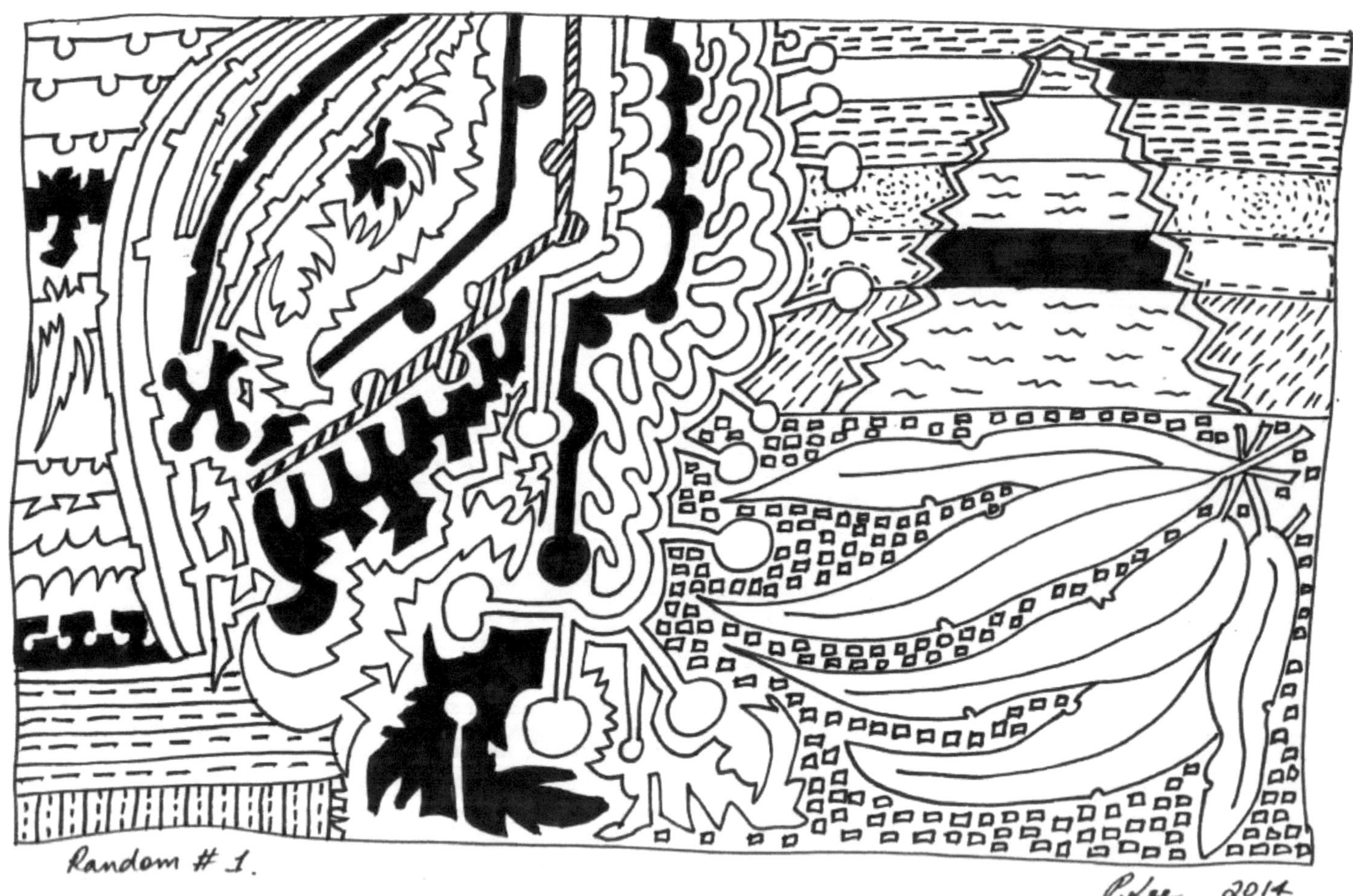

Random # 1.

P. Lee 2014

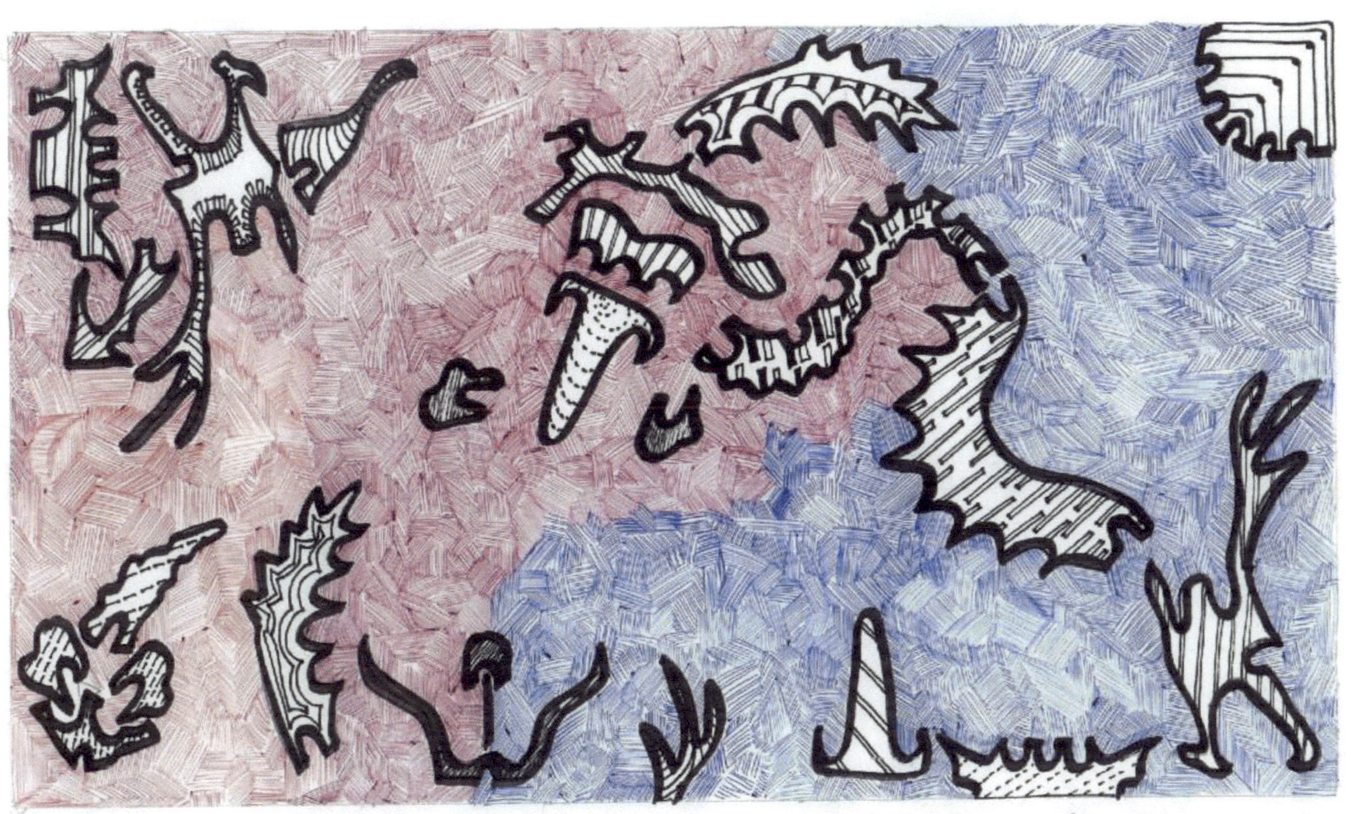

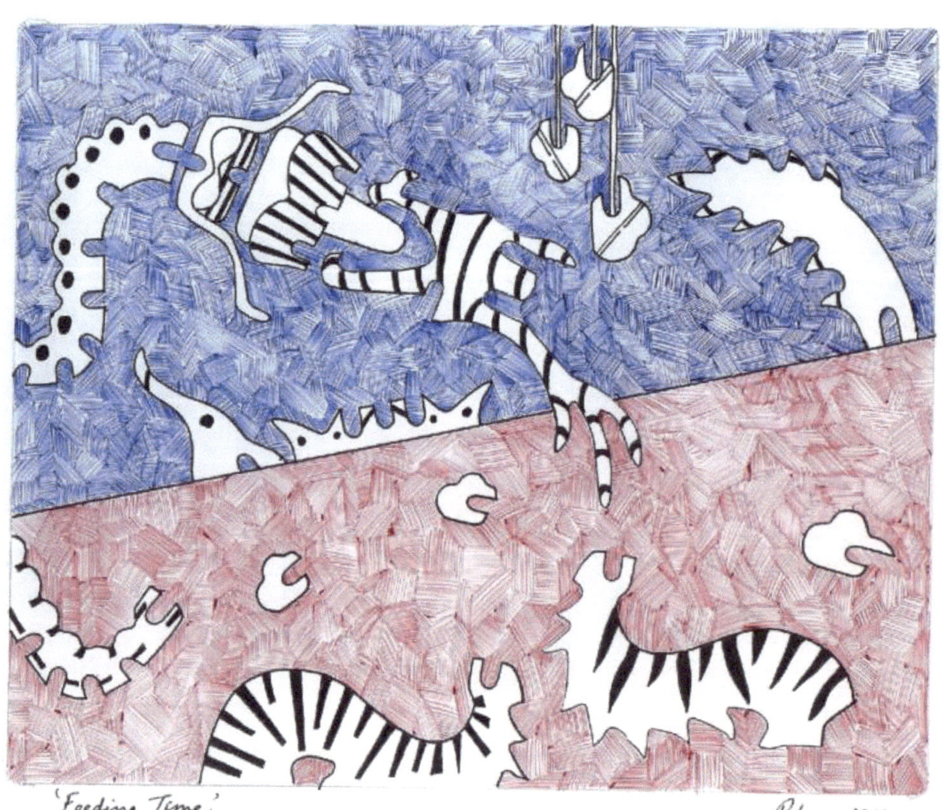

'Feeding Time'

P.Lee 2014

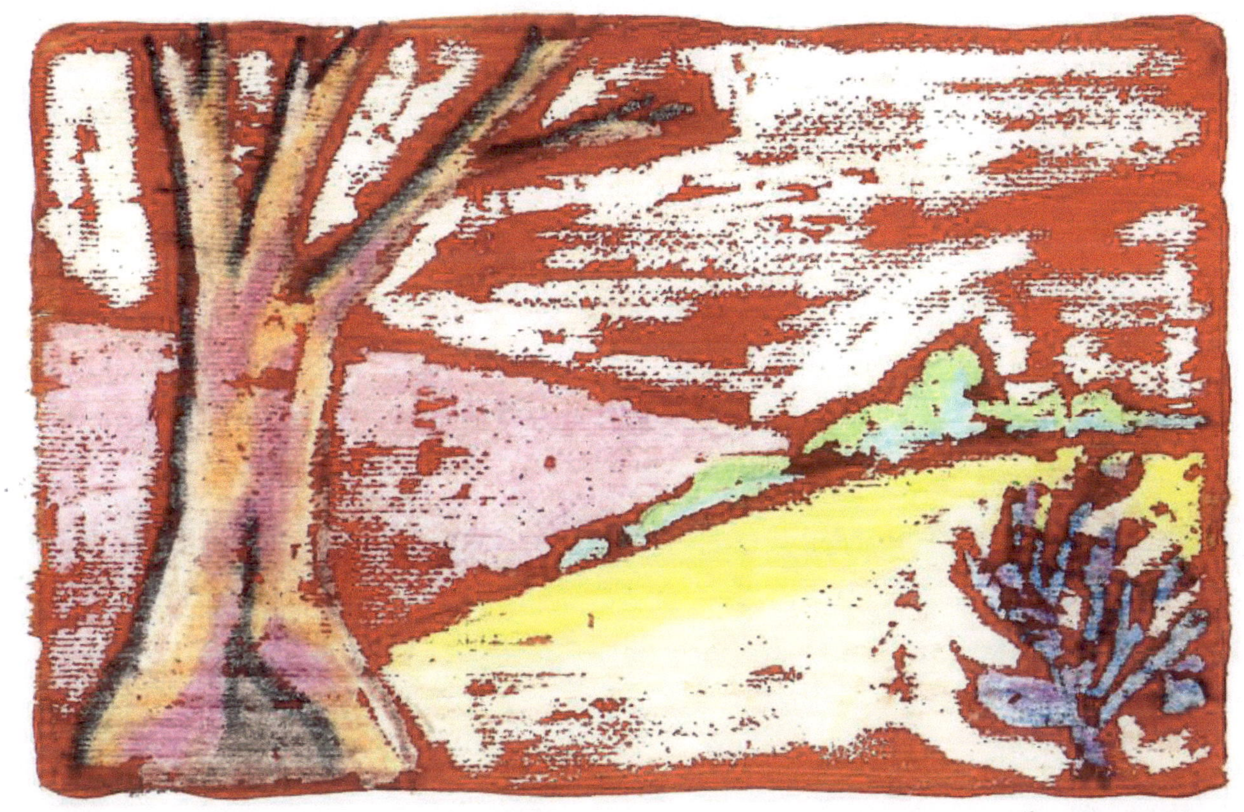

'Impression in Red'   PLee, 2016

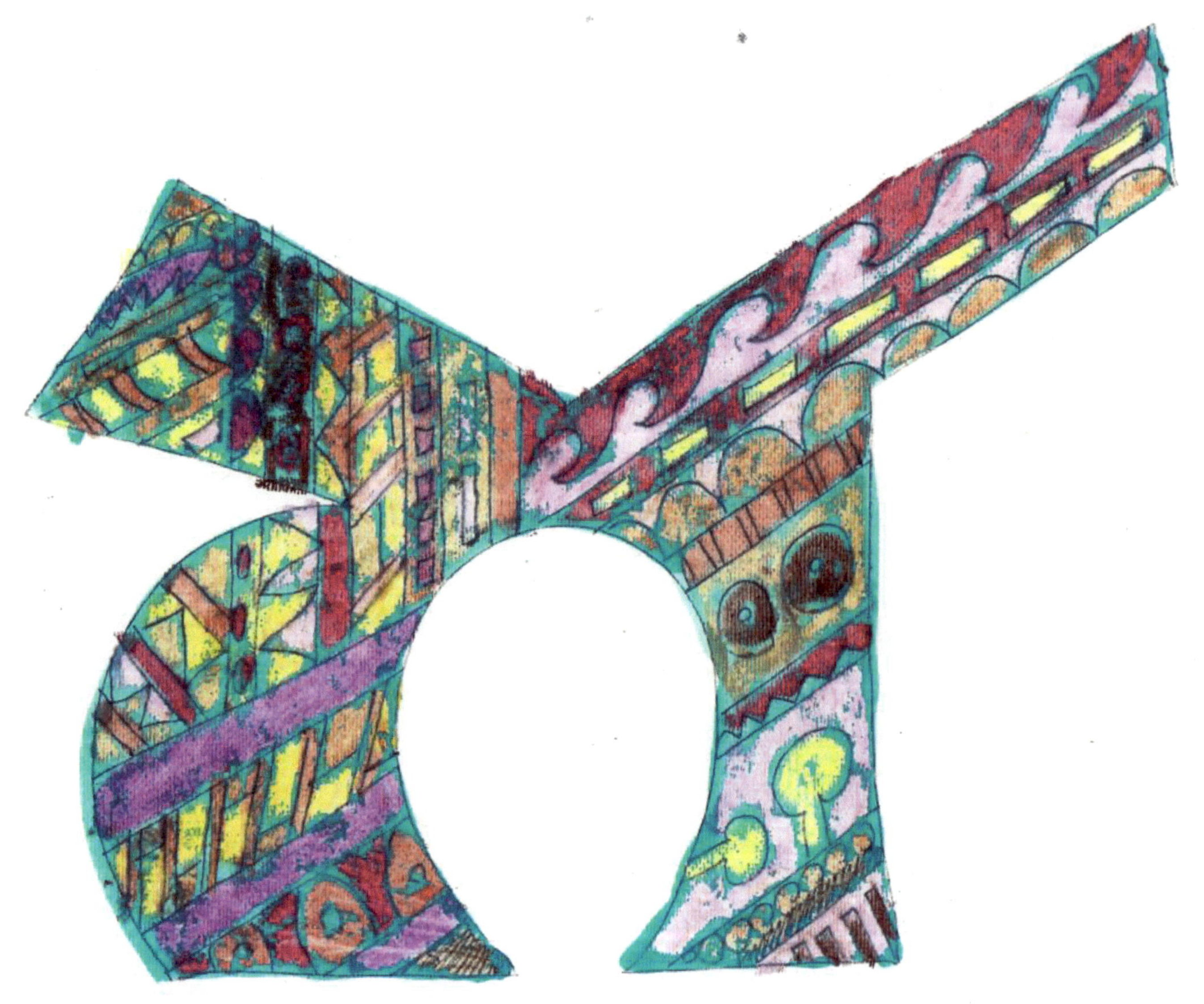

2016

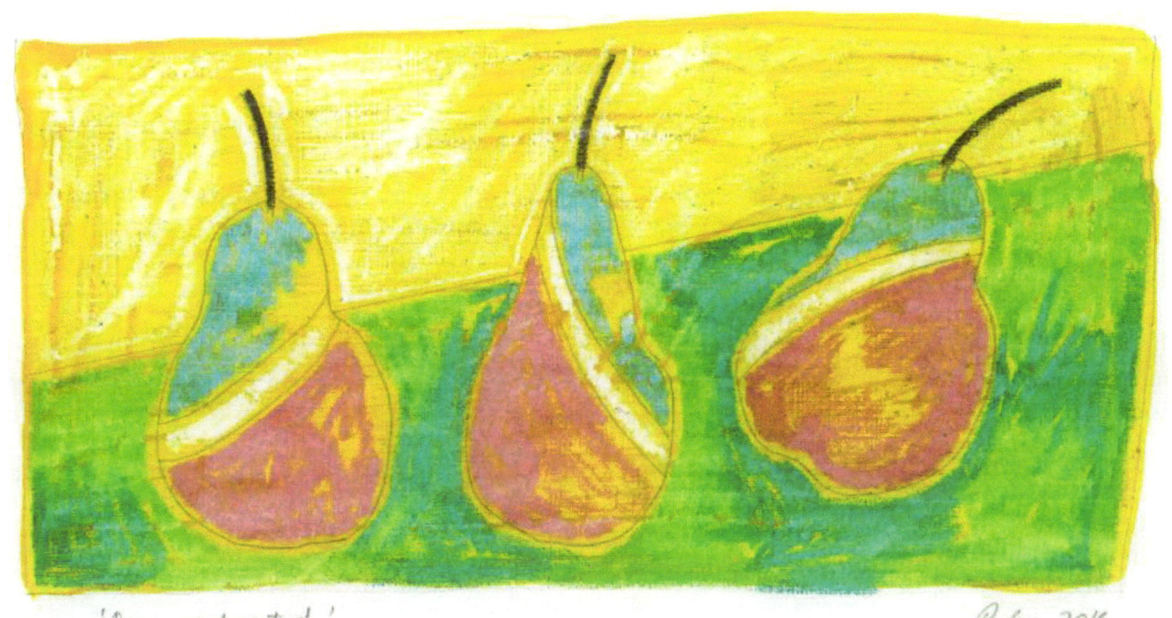

'Pears subverted'
P. Lee 2016

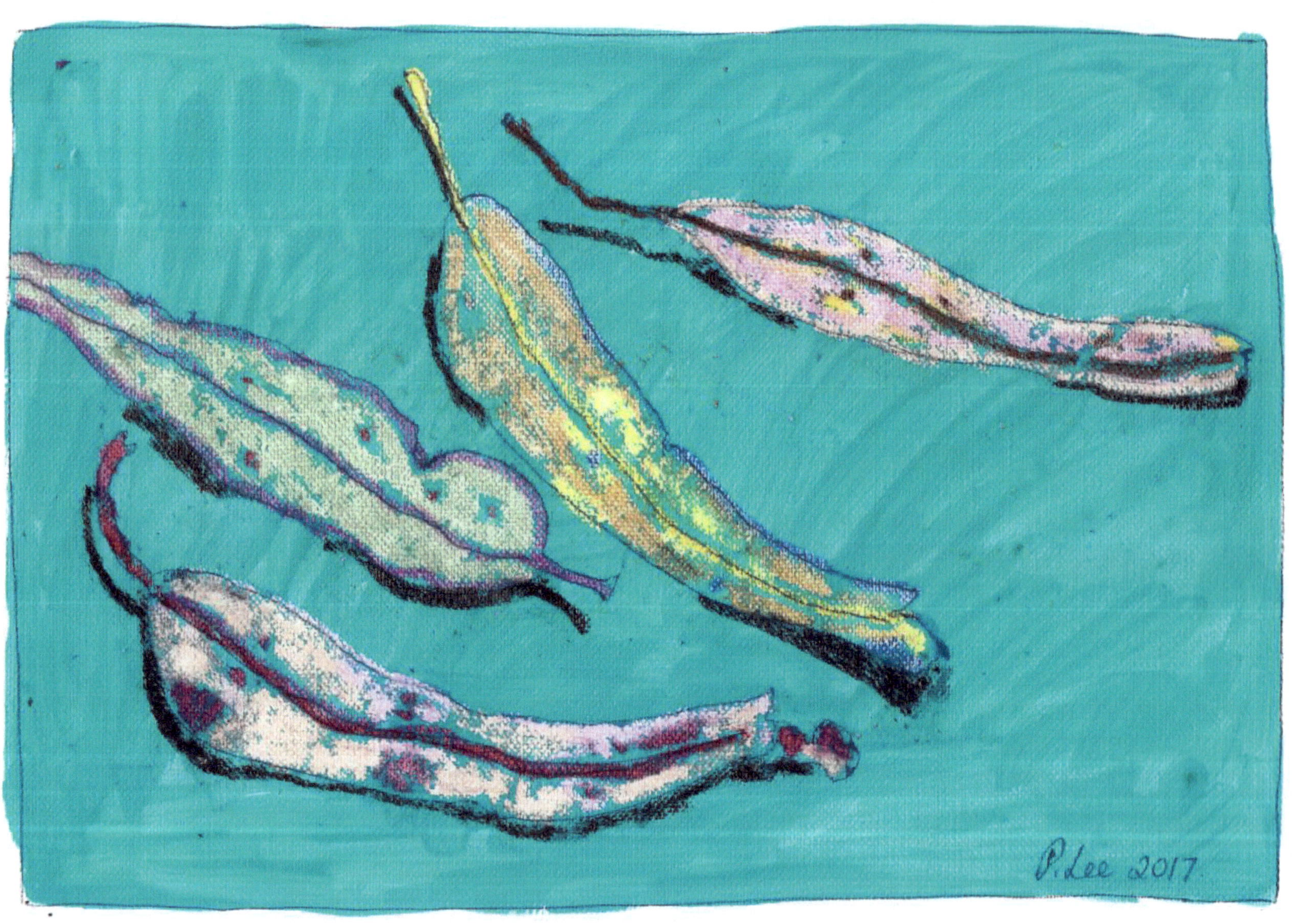

P. Lee 2017

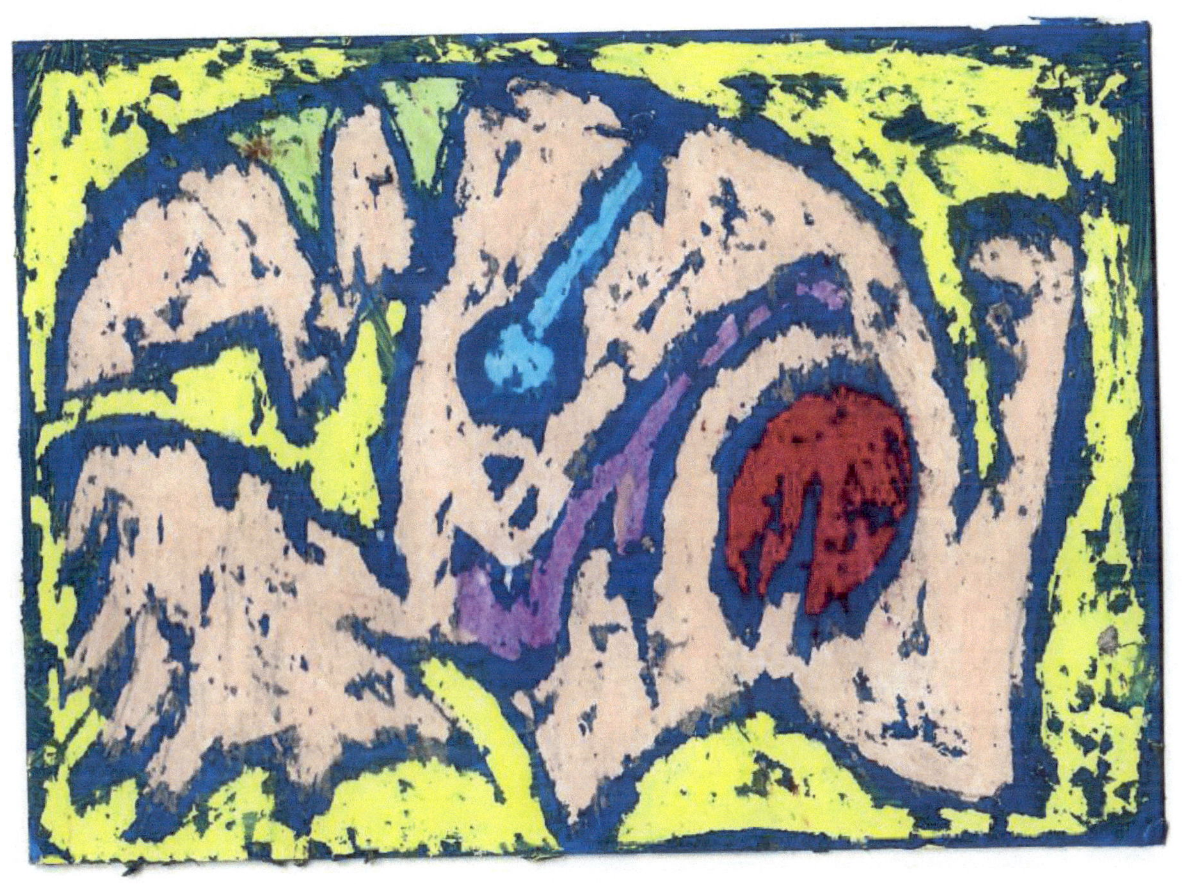

2017

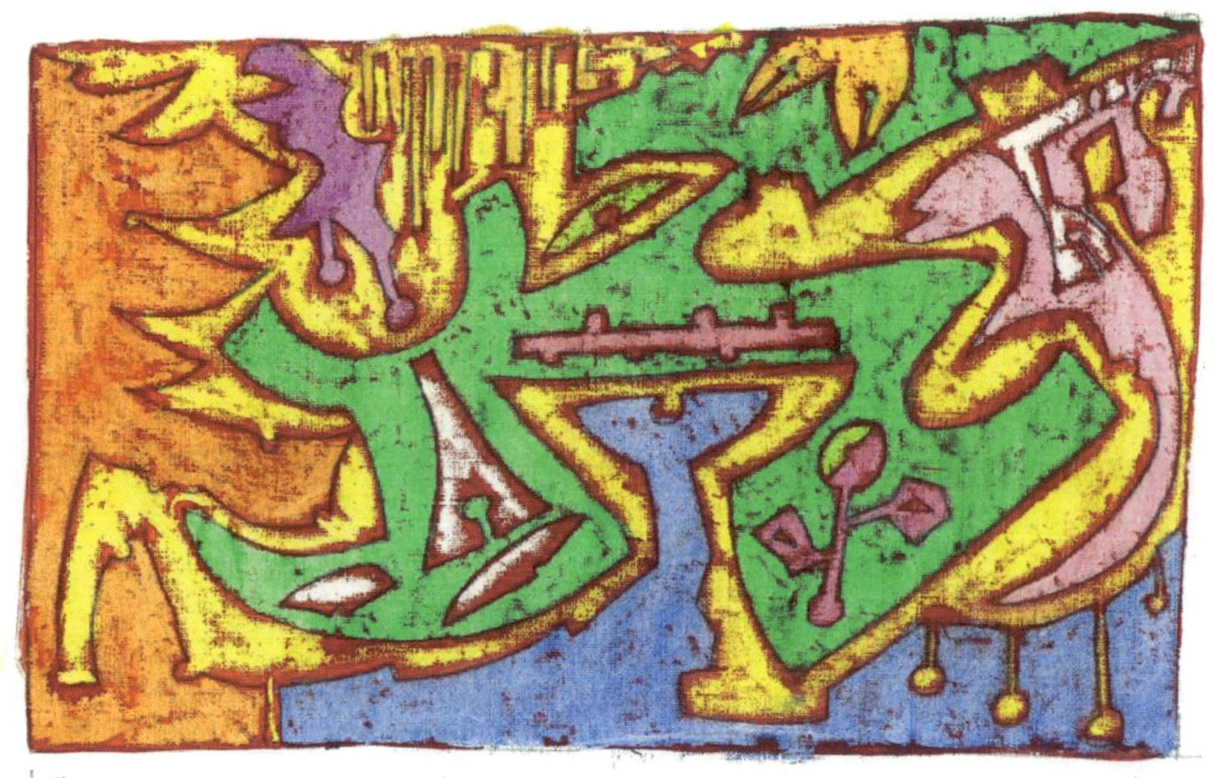

'The importance of upheavel'

P. Lee, 2018

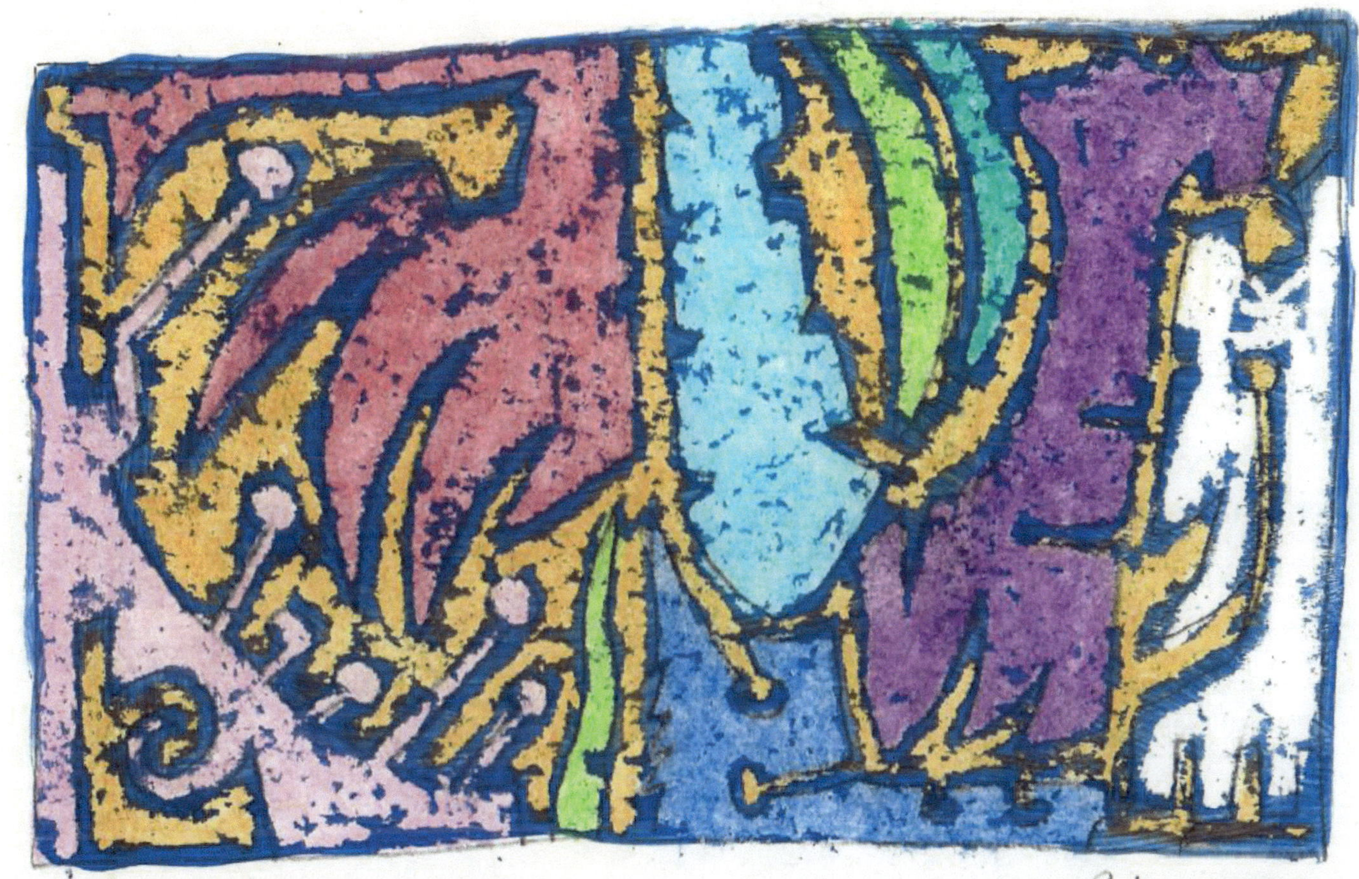

'Mellow crowd'
P. Lee 2018

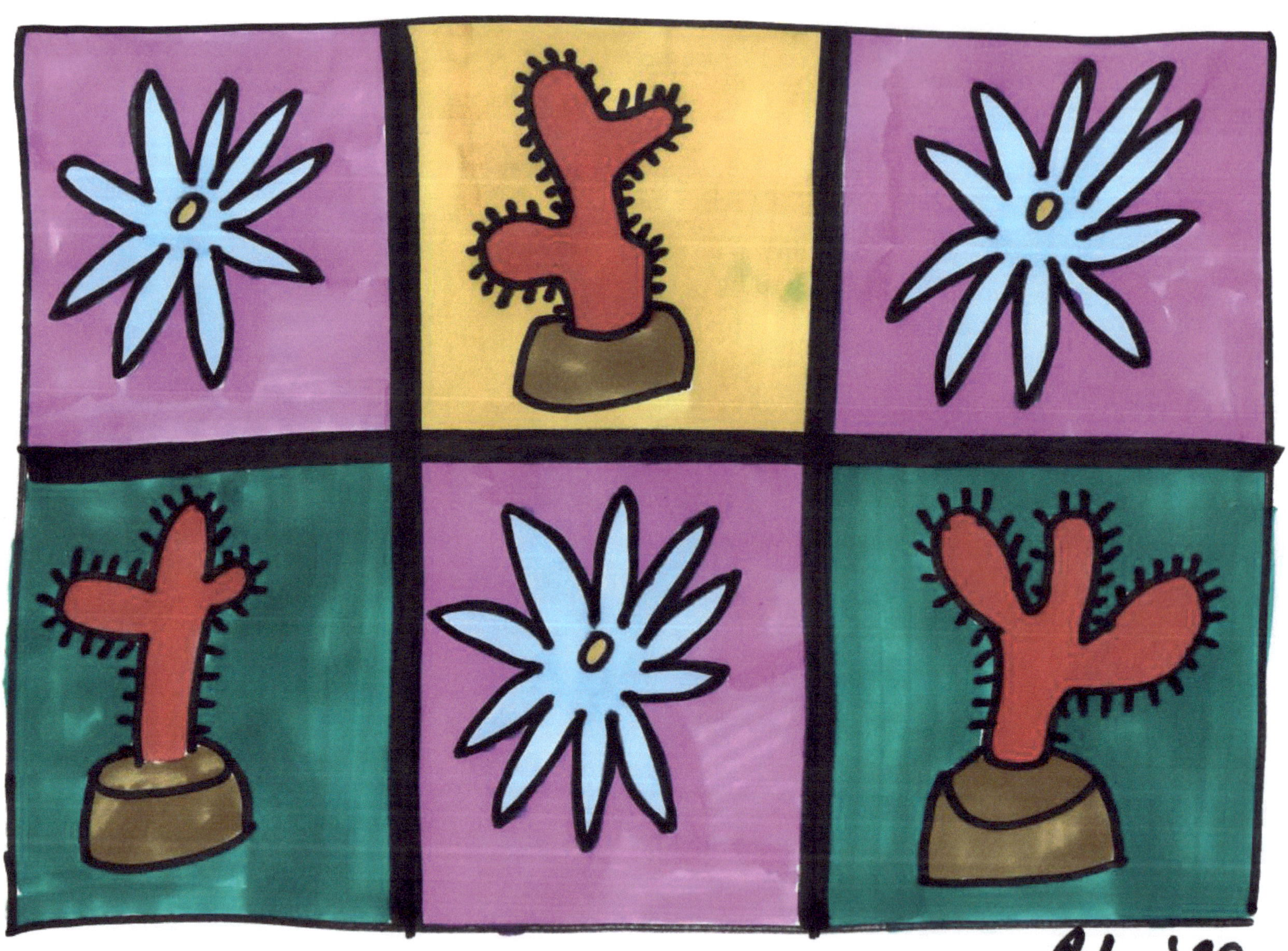

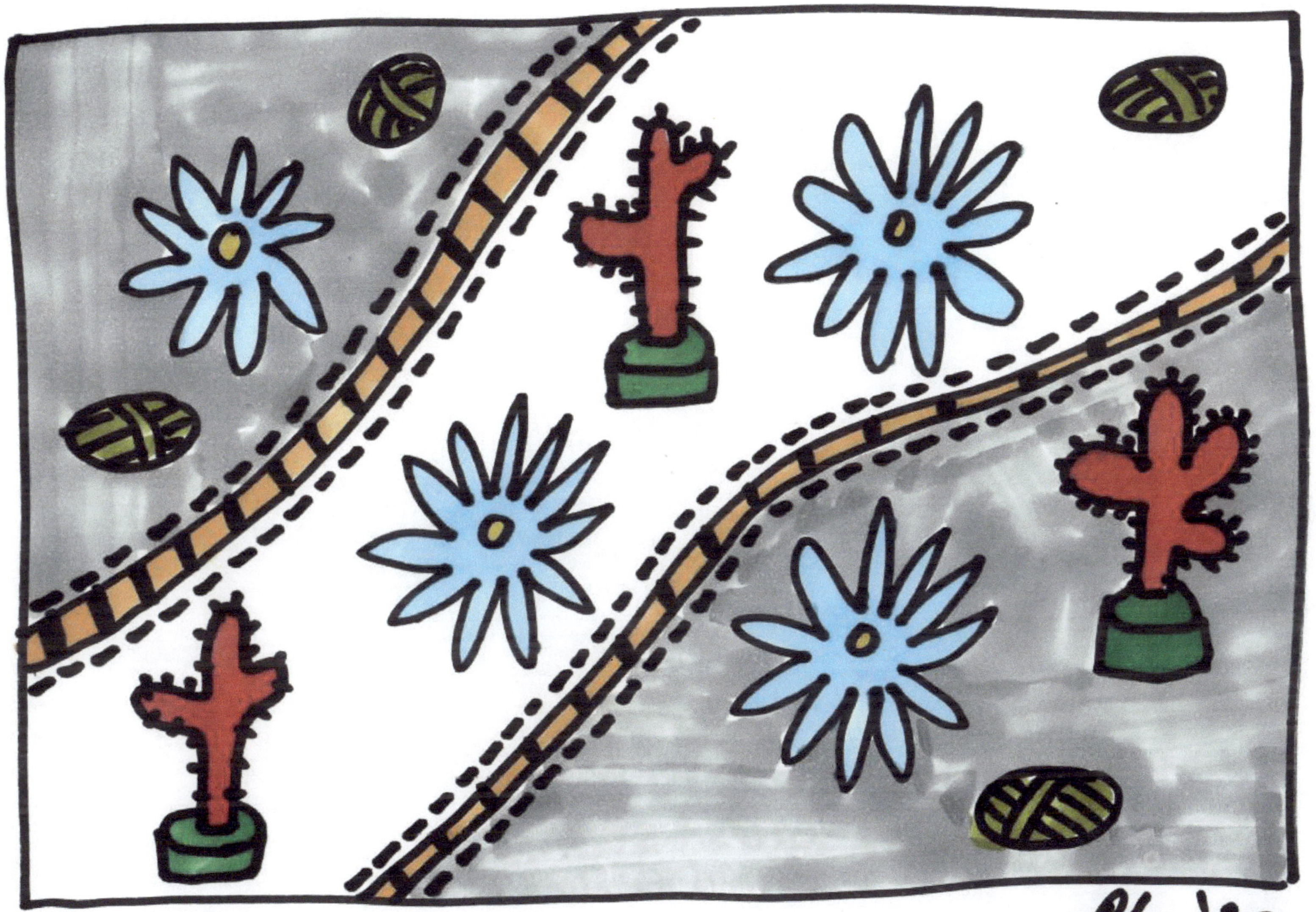

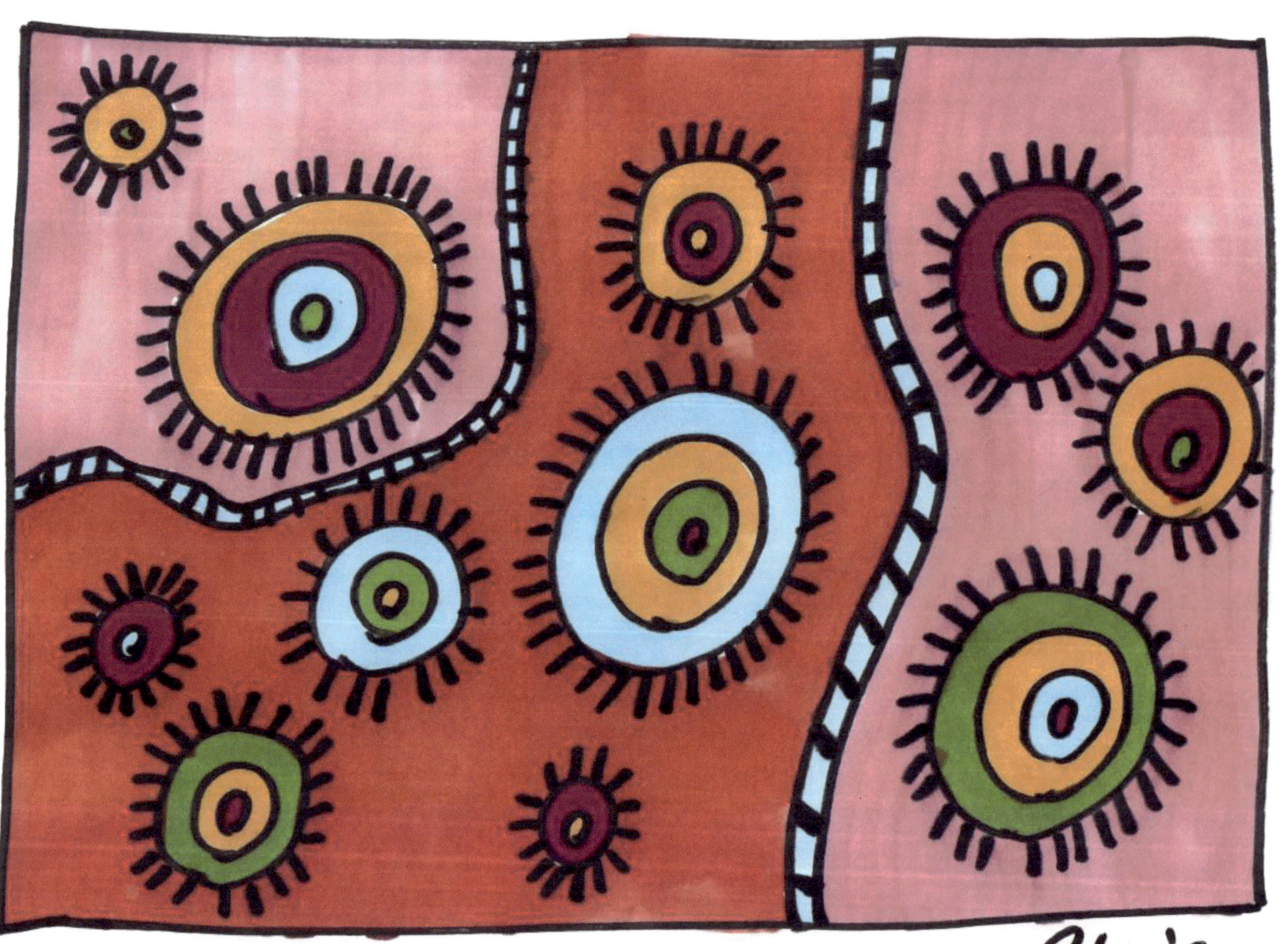
P.Lee '20

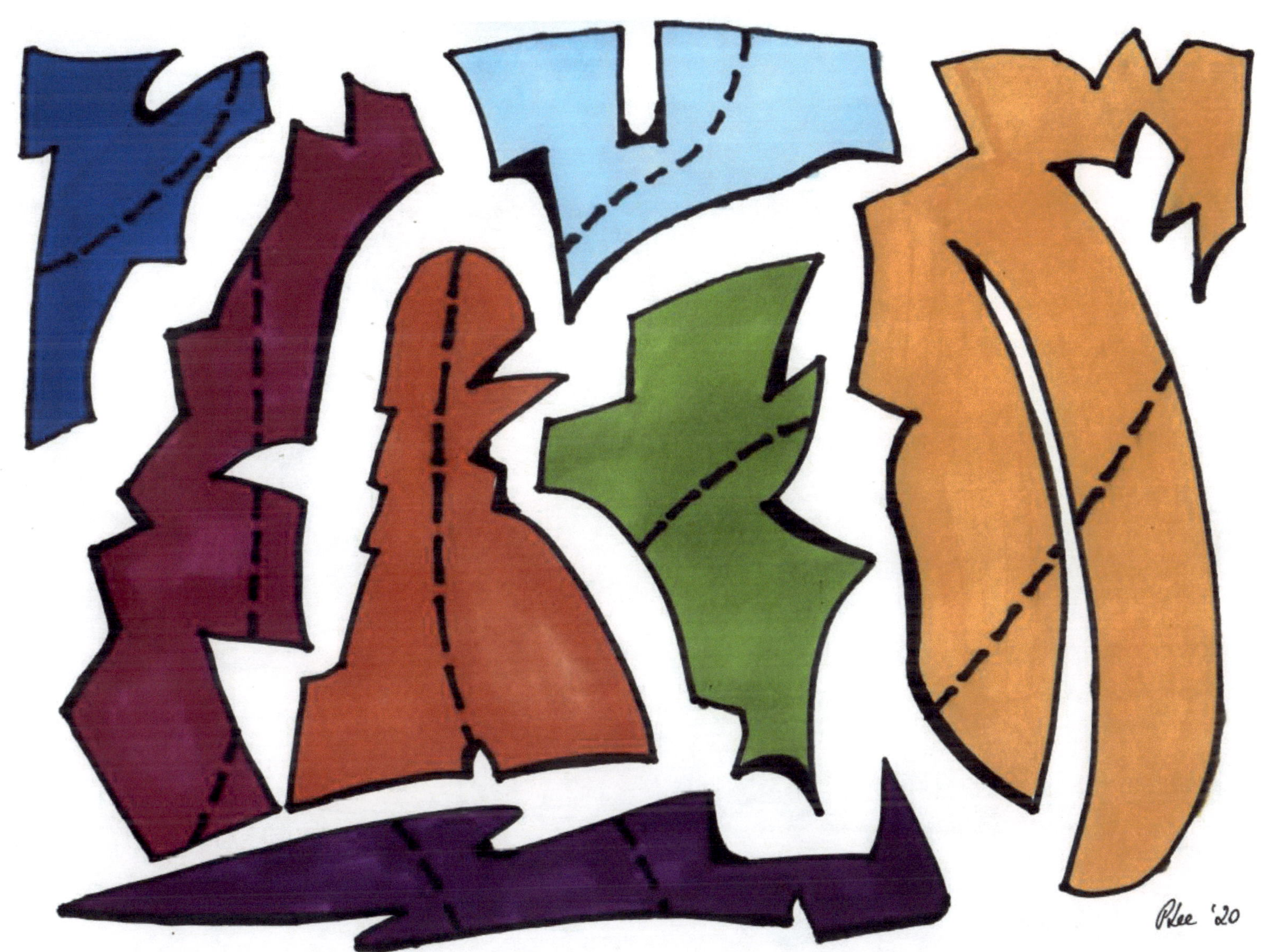

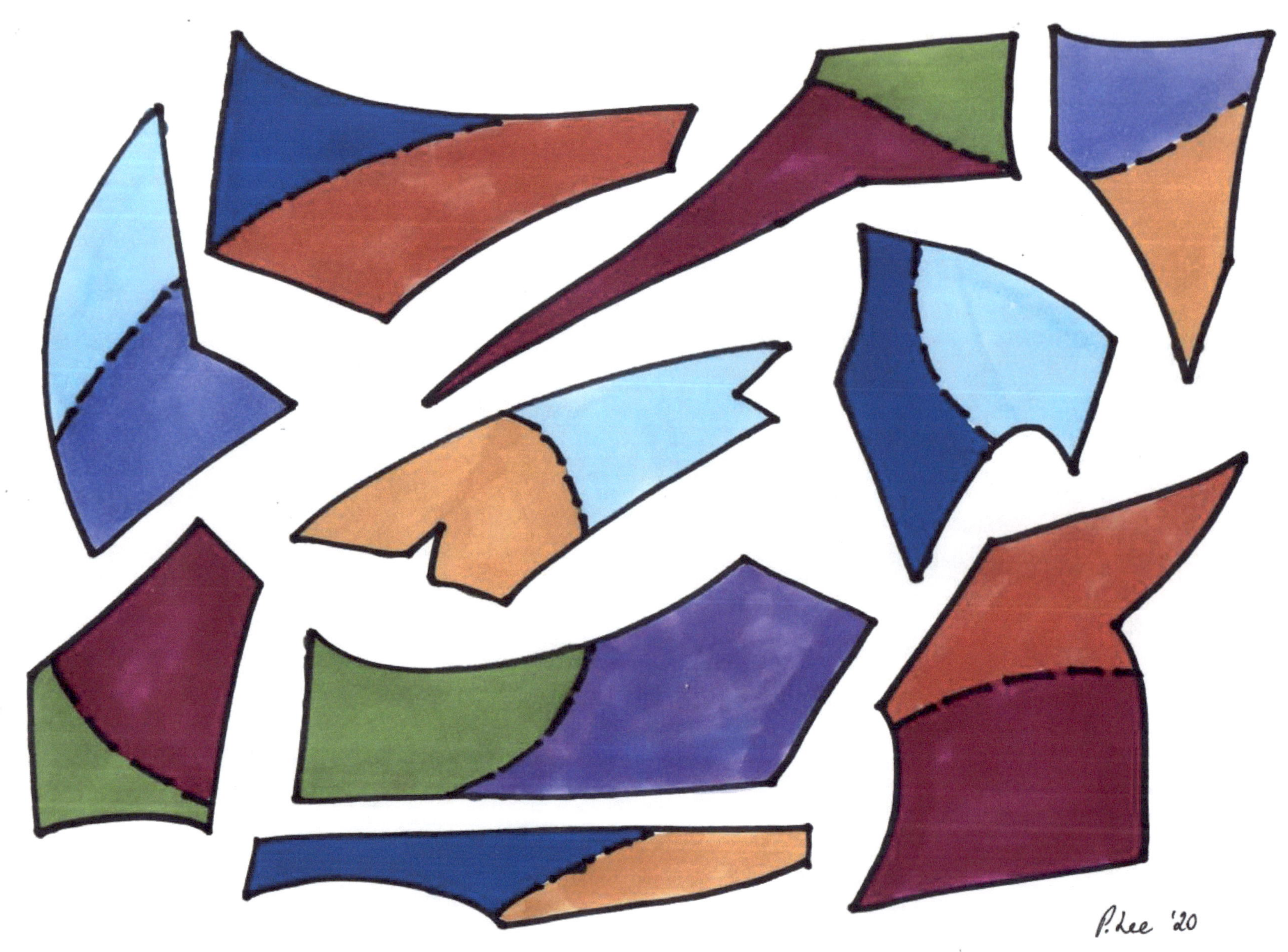

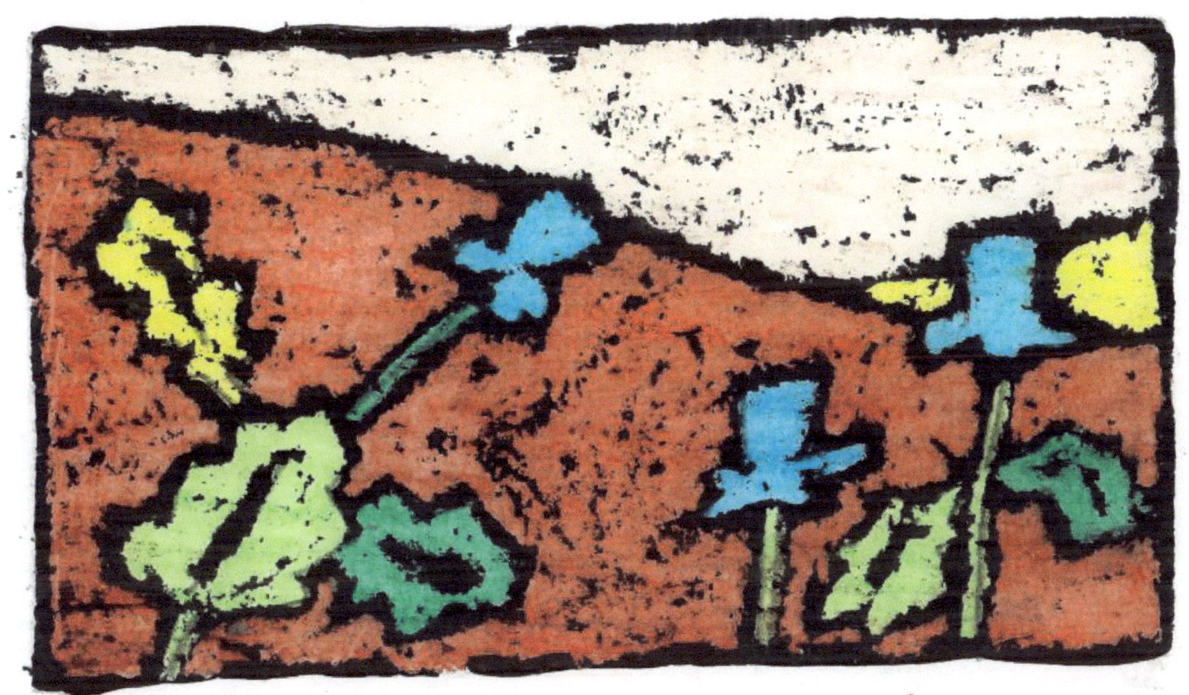

'Coming Together'
P.Lee 2022

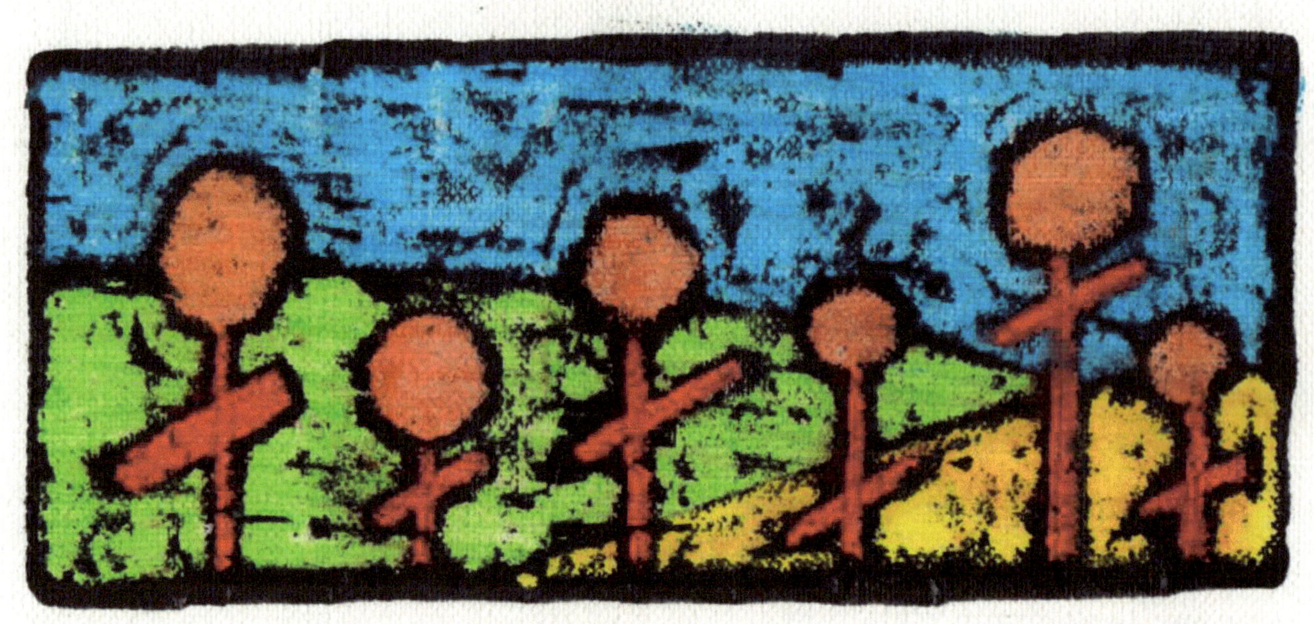

'For the Fallen'
P.Lee 2022

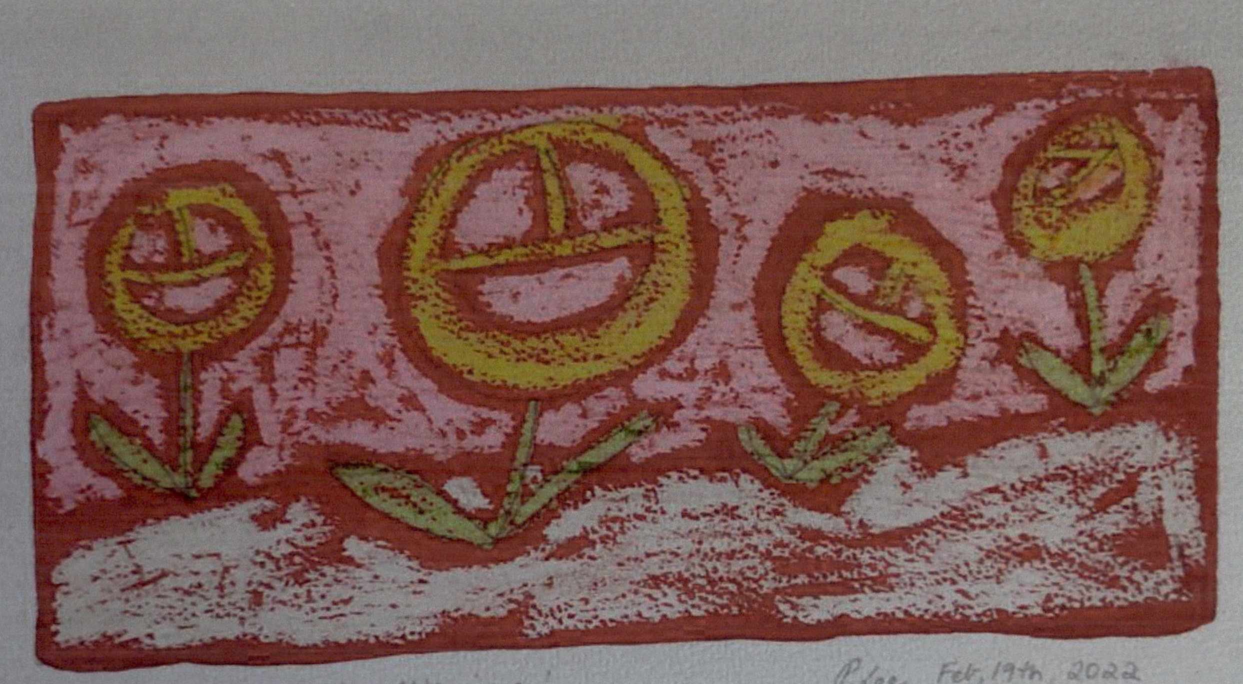

'No War in Ukraine'

P. Lee   Feb, 19th, 2022

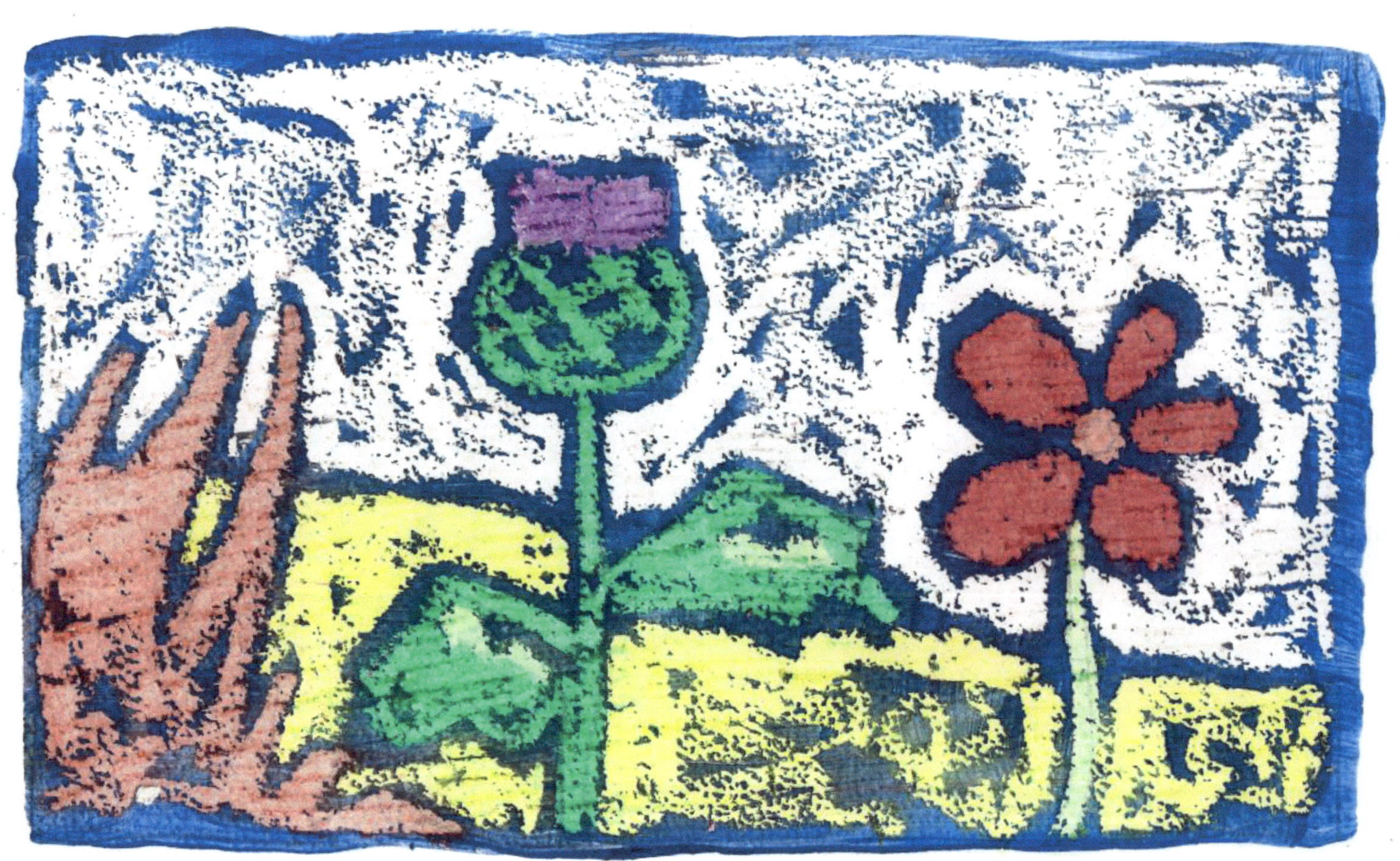

'Say hello to Mr Prickly' P Lee 2022

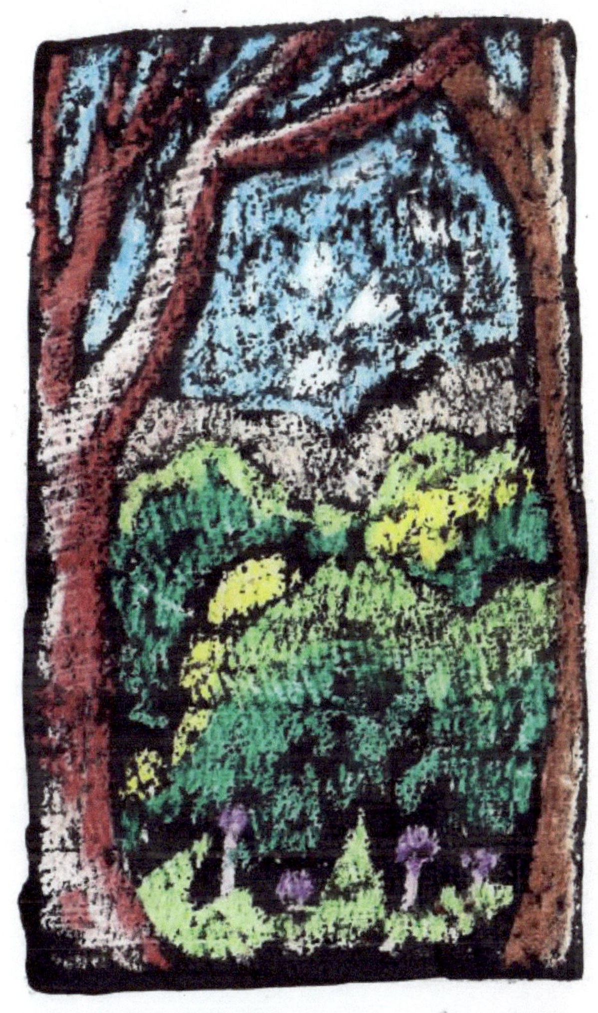

"Into the Forest   PLee 2022

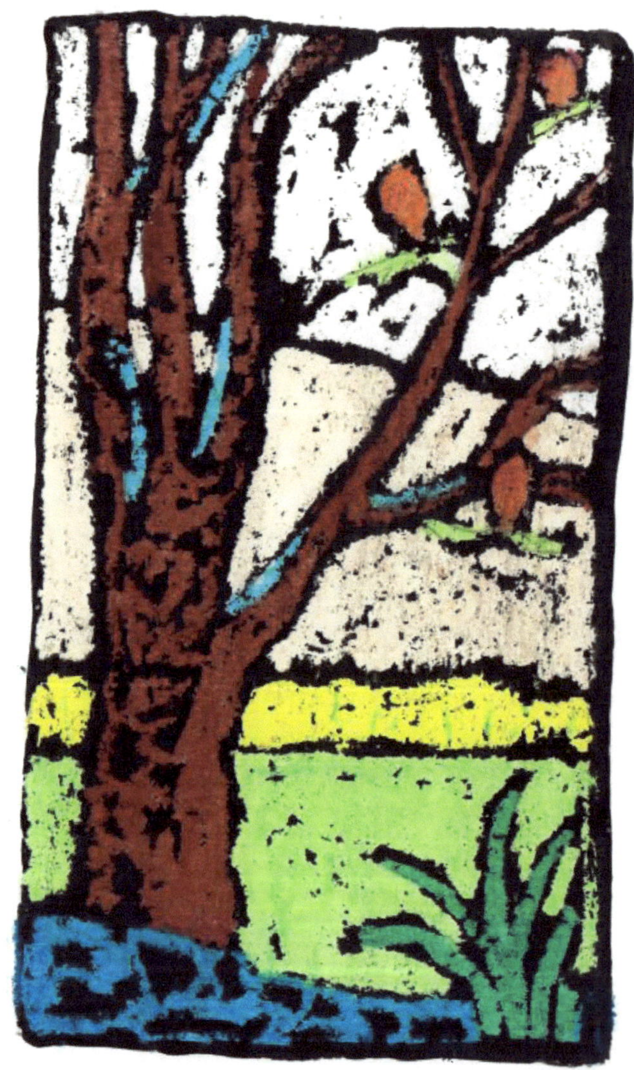

'The Return'
2022

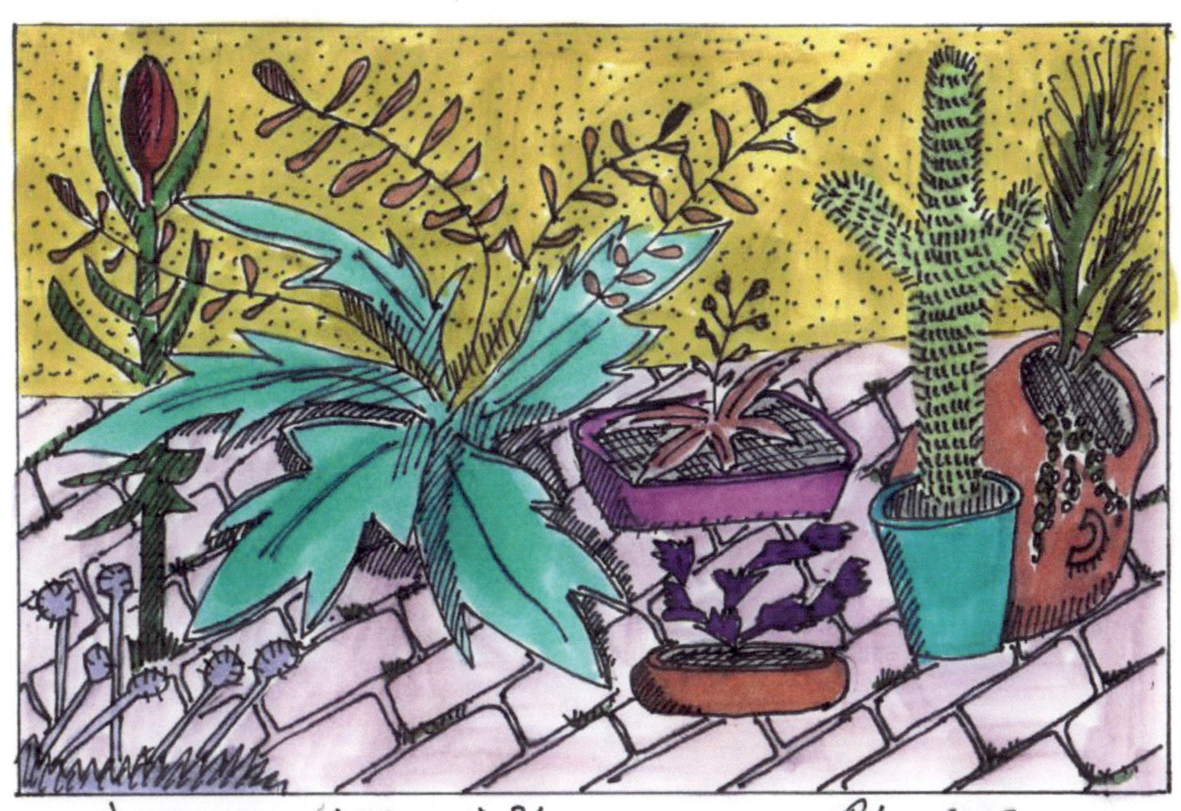
'Will the prickles win?'
P.Lee 2023

www.ingramcontent.com/pod-product-compliance
Lightning Source LLC
Chambersburg PA
CBHW042024050726
47602CB00010B/156